ROCKY MOUNTAIN
Pastels

ROCKY MOUNTAIN *Pastels*

EVIDENCE OF AN EXISTENCE

ROBERT ROBINSON

Copyright © 2016 by Robert Robinson

All rights reserved. No part of this publication may be reproduced, stored in a retrieval system, or transmitted, in any form or by any means, except as may be expressly permitted by the 1976 Copyright Act or by Robert Robinson in writing.

ISBN: 978-0-9972399-1-1

Printed by Createspace

Typesetting and cover design by www.wordzworth.com

Contents

Foreword
vii

One
Let There Be Trout
1

Two
The Life
23

Three
Fiddler's Green
55

Four
The Other Guy
79

Afterword
105

Acknowledgments
111

Foreword

This is a collection of light writings—pastels if you will—about fly-fishing in the Intermountain West, collected over thirty years of hiking and fishing, meeting good people, and picking at the wind-knots in my head.

Let There Be Trout

Nowhere In Particular

I leaned against the tailgate, watching the sun expose the flatlands below, wondering if I'd miss any of it. I'd breezed through Denver in the wee hours, instinctively not wanting to add to the fetid and festering flotsam that collects along the Front Range. I was heading *into* the mountains, away from humidity and sweat, away from those who lean on the brass bull and are defined by profits and stuff, away from those who would happily sell their mother's soul for a quart of beer and a twenty-rock. They are "the others," and I wouldn't miss *them*. I wouldn't miss home either. I'd never had one.

I'd attended fifteen different schools in five states before quitting high school to go into the service, so when people asked me where I was from, I'd answer, "Nowhere in particular." I'd owned property and lived out of my truck, been married and gotten divorced, played the game and dropped out. The only thing that had been a constant for me through it all had been fly fishing.

It was fly fishing for wild trout as much as a desire to put distance between me and the flatlands that drew me to the Intermountain West, the final destination of Hemingway, and the refuge of Wallace Stegner, Edward Abbey, and Harry Middleton—interminable drifters and seekers who'd found something out here in this bigness that reminds you to be small.

Hemingway found a shotgun—perhaps his ego wouldn't compress. Middleton found people living on the fringe of society who cared for him, a beautiful woman, and a blind trout. Stegner and Abbey found purpose in a love of land that sucked them into causes and battles. Stegner fought the damn dam builders and retreated to Vermont; Abbey stayed and continued the fight until his death; and Middleton took his memories back to Alabama, county garbage truck no. 2, depression, and a brain hemorrhage. The common denominator then was death, and I wondered if that's what *I* would find among these wind-scoured peeks. I'd come to catch wild trout in stream-gouged canyons and hold God in my hand. I found a land in trouble.

I met people able to strip mountains of their beauty for profit and leave with their hubris intact. I met people who'd lived here all their lives, looking up at the mountains every day, never bothering to go up there. Those that did go left a trail of beer cans, worm containers, and dirty diapers, striding through the land with a total disregard for anything but self. I couldn't go deep enough into the high country to escape corporate America, illegal gillnet operations, and the glint of empty beer cans. The federal government claimed some of the high ground, creating national forests, parks, and monuments in an effort to preserve as much of the land as they could.

But the flatland politicians don't like that, and they're making moves to declare that land state land. Their corporate buddies will pay big money to develop, drill, dig, and cut their way to greater wealth. The scars of scraping, digging, and over-grazing mark their trails, and blue exhaust hangs in the high-country canyons like fat on a bishop. They are embryonic gods, put here to "prosper on the land," destined to rule over their own planets and galaxies.

It took a while for my obsession with fly fishing to become more about the places it took me than about catching fish, and it wasn't until frantic bumbling turned to quiet competence, until manic passion gave way to quiet reflection that I started looking around. The passage of time etched into the khaki sandstone cliffs highlighted my puny life span, leaving me with a profound sense of my nothingness. The power that formed these mountains was hard to comprehend. These sweeping valleys surrounded by snow-covered peaks outlined against a hard blue sky made it impossible for me to think that *I* mattered, and I doubted if *any* of society's petty doings mattered.

I'd come west from the east, where impressive things are built, brick by brick, by people. But no earthmover, no economically enslaved civilization could build these mountains. The cliff faces told of their violent birth, the boulders in the valleys, of their constant change. No, people could not *build* mountains, but they *could* destroy them.

The mountains are under assault from corporations, environmentalists, outdoor enthusiasts, and ranchers. Corporations want to mine, log, and use the water for their cooling towers; environmentalists want to restrict access; outdoor enthusiasts want more access; and ranchers need to graze stock and water crops. And people need jobs.

All sides are convinced of the moral superiority of their respective positions, believing the other side to be either moon-bats, incapable of reasonable discourse, or robber barons, bent on the destruction of nature in the name of godless capitalism. There's some truth to both viewpoints, but neither side will own those inconvenient truths. Half-truth is more easily embraced, as whole truth is *always* messy. There are no all-satisfying solutions to any of this. It's a cluster.

The biggest fights in the West are over water. There's a saying out here: "Whiskey's for drinkin', water's for fightin' over." It's possible to be beaten or even murdered over water—it *is* the Wild West, after all—and everybody has a dog in the fight, old recluse fly fishermen included. The steely-eyed, quietly-moral westerner is a myth. A man's word means the same thing here as it does anywhere else—absolutely nothing. So instead of honorably tradin' lead, these battles are mostly fought with money and lawyers, the lawyers being the big winners. The losers? Wildlife, forests, and people. I realized the hopelessness of it all when I attended a function put on by a local conservation group.

I looked around the room and it was obvious these well-intentioned geriatric hippies didn't have the money to fight protracted legal battles, and short of going to the state capitol and setting their ponytails and beards on fire, they were unlikely to garner much attention to their cause. The guy we'd come to hear speak wasn't Edward Abbey, and as far as ground forces, well, there were no Haydukes in the crowd. The big money concerns are consolidated, the environmentalists divided, and ranchers in the West have *never* been able to agree on the color of scat. But they aren't the mountain's only enemies. Natural enemies can be just as destructive, and the forest service's trial-and-error methods of management—mostly errors—leave the mountains ripe for devastation that takes a generation from which to recover.

There's nothing sadder than hillsides covered in the dead brown and quiet gray of beetle-killed pines. Add drought, and you have a forest of powdery tinder primed for storms that bring little rain but plenty of lightning. Fires rage for weeks, leaving burn-scarred canyons, ash-covered streams, and bristling forests of blackened sticks. After a fire, the runoff sends walls of rocks, mud, and debris into the valleys, blowing out roads, choking off creeks, killing fish. They bring in heavy equipment to repair roads and open up streams, creating more problems. Seeing a D-9 Cat sitting in the middle of what was once a blue-ribbon trout fishery, leaking hydraulic fluid and oil is—well.

I'd come to the mountains to fish for wild trout and found refuge and a sense of purpose. I found quixotic battles, passed down by fallen legends, waiting to be fought. And I found indescribable beauty. For the first time in my life I noticed the wonderment around me. I caught myself looking up a lot, watching the wind whip ribbons of ice crystals from snow-covered peaks, and when that arctic air washed into the high valleys, I felt a cleansing—down deep. I understood why ancient people held mountains sacred. I would never have figured that out on the hot, muggy flatlands, and I knew I'd done good by coming here. I also knew I could no longer stand on a mountain, looking down, feeling smug. I now had an answer for the question, "Where ya from?" I wasn't from "nowhere in particular" anymore. And it no longer mattered *why* I'd come.

SOLITUDE

Fly-fishing is a solitary pursuit. The mechanics of the rod, the distances required between fly-fishers, and, of course, the grumpy nature of anglers preclude interaction. Most of my fishing buddies are family men. They go fishing in search of solitude and a break from the hassles of family life. I enjoy their company when we fish together, but our conversations invariably erode into shouting …

back and forth ... across the stream ... until we tire of trying to communicate and wander off to fish alone.

Henri Nouwen wrote, "Solitude is the furnace in which transformation takes place." In the furnace, the soul is hammered, tempered, and hardened; in the furnace, your demons are revealed, and you claim them and name them, as you would a child; in the furnace, you learn to tolerate your own company and become comfortable with yourself, in spite of yourself. But it's the loneliness of solitude that people fear, and many tragic mistakes are made in its avoidance.

Living in the Intermountain West, wilderness and the solitude it offers is only a thirty-minute drive in any direction, yet there are people who live here all their lives and never go to the mountains. The wild bigness of the mountains scares them, or maybe their demons are too monstrous.

Antoni Gaudi, the architect of the Basilica Sagrada Familia in Barcelona wanted the interior of his church to have the feel of a forest. He thought people feel closer to God in a forest. I think that is true. The facade of the Basilica reminds me of the small groves of pine that form just below the timberline where pine forests give way to aspen. When I look up at those piney spires, it's easy to understand how Druids came to worship trees and why we think of Heaven as being above.

My trips into the mountains are not initiated by a desire for the spiritual, but by a desire to fish; however, once I'm there, surrounded by the beauty of the mountains, I and my reasons become insignificant. I think of the thousands of years it took to form the mountains, the thousands of years they have stood, and the thousands of years they will stand after I'm gone. I consider my mortality, and the door of spiritual awareness swings open—I no longer fear going through. Up there, in those mountains, I've shaken hands with demons, stared into their ugly faces, took responsibility for them, and learned that

I'm not such a bad guy after all. And I consider myself a friend. The question isn't whether to go through the door, but whether the trout are taking dries.

For me, solitude is the natural order of things. Except for my dog, Touch, I live alone, and although we have conversations, they tend to be one-sided. Before I got Touch, I would go for months never speaking a word. I once startled myself with the sound of my voice. I was doing dishes and decided to make myself a sandwich. While spreading mayo onto a slice of bread, the bread flipped out of my hand and landed in the dishwater. I said, "Damn!" It was as if someone had shouted in my ear. I talk to Touch now, which keeps my vocal cords from becoming petrified.

I have fishing buddies who've invested in my solitary life style. They tell me I'm their hero. They think my solitary existence a heroic statement against the norm rather than the result of piss-poor choices and a desire to insulate myself from what had become a vicious cycle of pain and rejection. They don't realize that after twenty years of living alone, any rewards were long ago reaped. So when I told them that an old girlfriend from high school was coming for a visit, they shouted in unison, "You're screwed!" and slowly walked off shaking their heads (presumably to don sackcloth and sprinkle ashes on freshly shaven beans before heading home to their wives).

I don't have the gift of prophesy my friends have, so I don't know if my solitary existence will ever come to an end. Perhaps my solitude, like theirs, will someday *be* snatched in bits and pieces, but I know where to go to find it.

There's a small creek that runs through a narrow valley surrounded by green mountains. Nobody fishes it; they say the fish are too small. But they're the most brilliantly colored trout I've ever seen, which makes me think it's a special place, a place of healing, a place I would take a friend—a friend in need of solitude.

Etiquette

When I took up fly-fishing, I thought I had become a member of a club, a club of brother anglers, a club of gentlemen—men like Robert Traver and Nick Lyons. I thought I'd be embraced by kindly old gentlemen in tweed who would take me under their wings and give me fatherly advice. I would sit at the feet of sages, on lush, green riverbanks, in the shade of magnificent oaks, and the secrets of the sport would be revealed. I thought fly-fishing, courtesy, culture, and respect were synonymous. I was living in a fantasyland of bullshit.

When I hit the stream, I was rejected. My bib overalls, ditch boots, and thirty-dollar, fiberglass rod were like signs around my neck declaring me unworthy. I didn't look like a fly-fisherman, and it was clear I hadn't paid the initiation fee. When I saw a guy doping his fly and asked him what he was doing, he said, "Nothing." When I would walk up on other anglers, they would cup their flies in their hands to keep me from seeing what they had tied on. If I asked what they had tied on, they answered in Latin … Baetis … Tricos … like I knew what the hell that was. When I gave friendly waves to other fishermen, I got curt nods in return at best—when I wasn't totally ignored.

I knew not to jump ahead of somebody who was already fishing and to get below them, giving them the unfished water ahead. I knew to keep a low profile and give an angler a wide berth and not spook his pool when I did have to pass. I knew not to wade out and approach an angler who was in the act of fishing; however, I myself was rarely afforded these considerations. I learned that if I tipped over on the river, my fellow anglers were more likely to step over my body or rifle my belongings than offer any help.

I was making my way along a hillside on a river in central Utah when I hit a patch of scree and my feet shot out from under me. I went sledding and turtling on my back thirty feet and over a ten-foot embankment into the river, landing on my butt with half the hillside, making a huge splash about ten feet from two anglers. One of them rushed over—I thought to see if I was okay—and with veins sticking out on his neck and eyes bulging shouted, "HEY! WE'RE TRYING TO FISH HERE!"

There's a stream that I love to fish because it's close to the house and access is easy. It has plenty of turn-outs along its course, and it's easy to spot other fisherman and stay out of their way. So, I was surprised one day when I rounded a bend in the creek and ran into fifteen anglers, along with a river guide conducting a fly-fishing class. The guide had a net strung across the creek and was giving a lesson on entomology. The little turn-out where I parked had ten vehicles in it, and I was blocked in and couldn't leave. All the guys were shiny, with unstained hats, unrepaired waders, and creases still in their vests. You needed sunglasses to look at them. They had their vests stuffed with stuff, which they would lose the first time they tried busting through the willows, and I thought if I followed them for a while, I'd make a killing on eBay. I walked up to the group and stood there until I got the instructor's attention, then asked, "When are you giving the lesson on stream etiquette?"

I have a fishing buddy who is the Crabby Appleton of fly-fishing. If he runs into another fisherman on the stream, it ruins his whole day. He refers to the movie *A River Runs Through It* as "that movie" and blames it for the crowds of fisherman it encouraged to take up the sport. If somebody asks him how the fishing is, he'll say poor, even if he had a fifty-fish day. If somebody asks him where he's been fishing, he'll lie and misdirect them to someplace where the fishing sucks. He was fishing a sweet bend pool on the Provo one day when he heard a splash behind him. He didn't see anything and figured it was a fish jumping, but when it happened again he started looking around and spotted a guy on the hill above him in the act of throwing a rock into his pool. The guy was a fishing guide who had a couple of sports he wanted to put on my friend's fishing hole. My friend reeled in and climbed up the bank to where they were standing and suggested that the guide had been having sexual relations with his own mother. When that failed to produce a response, my friend slapped him across the face with his handmade, bamboo fly rod and called him a punk. The look on the faces of the sports was priceless.

When a friend of mine told me one morning as we were stringing up our rods that his eighty-year-old grandmother had asked him to bring her a fish, I didn't give it much thought. He's been a catch-and-release fisherman for as long as I've known him. Keeping a fish for his granny wasn't going to hurt a damn thing. When he landed the one he wanted to keep and was in the act of creeling it, he was accosted by two anglers with shouts of, "Let it live!" and "Put it back!" He was so embarrassed that he reeled in and went home. I quit trying to explain my preference for catch-and-release a long time ago. I don't have a problem with people who keep the fish they catch, as long as the fish aren't wasted, and they're caught legally; however, I do have a problem with those who equate keeping a fish for your granny to murder.

Over the years I've found myself trekking farther into the backcountry in order to avoid the crowds. Unlike Crabby, it doesn't ruin my day to run into a fellow angler. I've met some super guys on the stream, developing friendships that are now decades old. I met a nice guy just the other day. His gear was shiny, and he was obviously new to the sport ... so I cupped my fly in my hand when he walked up.

Getting Lost

What I love most about fly-fishing is getting lost in the different aspects of the sport, forgetting about everything but the immediate problem of how to catch fish. I often tell myself (mostly when I'm not catching fish) that it isn't the catching of fish that's important—but it is. It's the only indication that of all the things you could've done wrong, you did them right. You don't have to be a fly-fisherman to leave your troubles behind when fishing, but sitting on a bucket, staring at a bobber, waiting for a fish to find stink bait leaves a guy with a little too much time to think. That would have *me* reaching for a bottle. And a gun.

The escape that fly-fishing offers is in the focus required to be successful, and for me this starts with the planning stages of a fishing trip, in choosing where I want to fish and which rod I want to use. I may have a rod that I've neglected, or one that's a particular favorite I need to reconnect with. There may be a piece of water that's been nagging, whispering, pulling me to return. I'll start daydreaming about what that water looked like the last time I was there and what it might look like now.

Depending on the time of year, I can make a reasonable guess as to stream conditions. I live in the Rockies, and in the spring the water changes daily, going from crystal clear to terrapin-turd brown. In summer, after runoff, choices of where to go and what to use can be made with more certainty; however, when I get to the stream, I often find my prior headwork undone. In spring, the water can be put off color by runoff washing sediment down from the mountains;

in summer, a stream can be clouded by passing thunderstorms. These showers can be localized, affecting one side canyon while leaving another untouched, causing only a small section of a creek to change color. If there has been a recent burn in a side canyon, or network of canyons, the effect on a stream can be extreme—even dangerous. It's surprising how little rain it takes to send a ten-foot wall of water rushing down a burn-scarred canyon.

If the water is only slightly cloudy, I'll fish it, but if I can't see the bottom and debris is flowing down, I find somewhere else to fish. I have a rule—if I can't see the bottom, I don't wade. When the water is murky, you can step in a hole, go in over your head, and get swept downstream with the rest of the trash. Sometimes creeks may be clear but running at a high level, and that can make for some good fishing, but crossing the stream to get into casting position when the water is high and fast will definitely keep your mind off your troubles.

When the water is running higher than normal, a familiar stretch of water looks unfamiliar. What was a nice riffle with well-defined feeding lanes now has no distinguishing features, and what was a back eddy is now part of the main current. But reading water is reading water; the back eddies and riffles are still there, they've just moved, and the fish are still there, they've just moved to new feeding lanes where they expend less energy to stay in position.

I check the weather reports the night before trips into the mountains, looking at wind speed and direction. Once I have an idea of the wind conditions, I make my final choice of destination and chose the rod I think will work best. Knowing what kind of wind I am likely to face gets me thinking about leader length and weight.

Besides the wind, whether or not the day is sunny or overcast determines length of the leader and tippet weight. On bright sunny days, trout are likely to see you coming before you can get within casting distance, making a longer cast necessary, requiring a longer leader. A combination of bright sunlight and clear water may make lighter tippet material desirable. If planning the trip, checking wind charts, choosing rods, leaders, and tippets hasn't gotten your mind off your troubles, deciding what fly to use when you get there will probably do the trick.

The idea that you're trying to fool fish with artificial representations of natural aquatic insects will necessitate even the casual fly fisher to become a half-assed entomologist. Learning what insects are likely to be present on a given stream at a particular time of year and at what stage of development can seem beyond the ability of a country boy, but you quickly learn to reduce the long Latin names to the one- and two-word names of the artificial patterns that represent them. The different stages of most riparian insects can be reduced to two: the nymph, or underwater stage, and the hatched adult fly. The kinds of flies used for fishing can be reduced to four: the stone, caddis, mayfly, and terrestrial. (Terrestrials are insects that live out their lives on dry land: crickets, ants, and grasshoppers.)

To represent these flies, thanks to generations of flytiers and their nefarious pattern recipes, there are hundreds of artificial flies to choose from. Of course, you can sink into depravity, tying your own flies, concocting your own evil recipes, and naming them after your ex-wife—The Dirty Alice. I know old-timers who've fished all their lives using one fly (the Double Renegade) and they catch a lot of fish, so it really isn't all that complicated.

When choosing a fly, I do go through the ritual of shaking willow bushes to see what flies are hiding there, straining the creek with my aquarium net to see what's in the water, and pawing through my flybox looking for a match before tying on an Adams. I'll sometimes tie a dropper nymph to the hook-bend of my dry fly; it's a good way to see what the trout are up to. But being a dry-fly purist, I make sure nobody's around when I do that.

Although I have plenty of commercially tied flies in my box, it's more fun to use the ones I tie myself. Tying flies is an excellent way to occupy the mind during those long winter months of being cooped up in the house, when you, the dog, and the old hides you're using to tie the flies all start stinking in equal measure. As spring approaches and fly boxes have been replenished, I begin playing with the traditional patterns, coming up with my own versions. Most commercial flies are tied in Taiwan now, but I still run into locally tied flies in little out-of-the-way fly shops, and I'll usually pick up a dozen or so to help the guy out. I also tie my own leaders and enjoy experimenting with their different formulas.

Casting is another aspect of the sport that has its devotees. Some people compete in casting competitions and hardly ever go fishing. I'm not a great caster. I only have a few casts mastered well enough to get by. Once I learned how to adjust the plane of my cast to avoid obstacles behind me, my life became much easier—as long as I remembered to look behind me first. I use the traditional forward cast and roll cast mostly, but the reach cast and single haul cast are handy tools to have in your bag of tricks, as well. Then there's the actual act of fishing itself to focus on, and everybody has their own ideas on how to fish.

I try to fish from the left side of a creek, moving along slowly, casting tight to the left bank with a forward cast, then working the fly across with a series of roll casts until landing the fly next to the right bank. I find a roll cast delivered upstream at a forty-five degree angle toward the right bank has enough built-in mend to give the fly a long drift without having to mend the line, and, for me at least, it works better than the reach cast.

Every aspect of the sport presents the angler with opportunities for getting away from the daily grind. From making your own rod and tying your own flies and leaders, to learning all the casts and how to read water, you'll find books written by experts on every facet of the sport. You can take it as far as you wish. You can take it too far. You can take it just far enough ... to get lost.

The Obsession

My mother was the fisherman in the family. The ol' man wasn't into it, so fishing trips were few and far between. But when we did go, Mom was all business, starting her preparations the night before by making her special bait/dough balls. I don't remember her exact concoction—I wish I did. Anyway, the dough balls weren't for the fish, they were for the crawdads that she used for bait to catch the fish. She would clean the crawdads down to tail meat, and using cane-pole, bobber, and hook she caught a lot of fish.

The old man sat on the bank reading a book while Mom baited and tended her fish poles. He never got *his* hands dirty cleaning crawdads, or landing and cleaning fish. Mom would have three or four poles going at a time, moving up and down the river bank, catching and cleaning crawdads, baiting hooks, and landing catfish. It was her thing. When we were at the river, she stayed focused, and it was best to stay out of her way. If you did anything to scare the fish (throwing rocks in the water, making loud noises), that was your ass. It must have been her that showed me how to thread a worm onto a hook, as I had that sticky operation firmly planted in my head the first time I saw a guy fly-fishing on TV. I asked my dad, "What kinda fishin' is that?"

Looking up from his paper, he said, "Fly-fishing."
"What do they use for bait?"
"Flies."
"How do they get them to stay on the hook?"
"They tie them on."

I had a vision of trying to tie a house fly to a fishhook, which seemed to me like a messy, tedious operation, so I gave fly-fishing no more thought until one foggy Sunday morning twenty years later.

I was heading home through the North Georgia Mountains after spending the weekend helping a friend with a historical preservation project. The sun hadn't been up long enough to burn off the fog, and visibility was zilch. I was creeping along when I spotted a guy fly-fishing a pond not far off the road and pulled over to watch. The fog obscured the man from the waist down. The tip of his rod disappeared into the fog's blank canvas above, the fly line vanishing … then reappearing to the rhythm of his cast. Very pretty. After watching him land a couple of fat bluegills, I walked over to get a better look at what he was doing. He was standing at the end of a dock that projected into the middle of the pond. I walked out to him just as he added another nice fish to his stringer. "Those are some nice fish." I said.

"Yeah, I think that's enough for breakfast," he replied. We talked about fishing and he showed me the fly he was using—a yellow and black bee looking thing—and gave me a quick casting lesson. I was hooked. I was just as hooked as the fish he was taking home for breakfast. I stopped at a sporting-goods store on the way home and bought a fly rod, reel, line, and some flies. From that point on, if I wasn't fly-fishing, I was daydreaming about fly-fishing, reading about fly-fishing, and wishing I was fly-fishing.

I bought every book on fly-fishing I could lay my hands on, and I learned that I needed more stuff. I needed a fishing vest—one with lots of pockets—to put all the stuff in. I needed more and better fly rods. I needed hip waders and chest waders. I needed a tying vise and tying materials. And, eventually, I needed marriage counseling and a good lawyer. I was obsessed (some said possessed), driven (the paperwork said psychotic), and one-track-minded (I prefer focused).

I went to all the fly-fishing meccas and began hanging out at fly shops, where I listened and learned about the life cycle of aquatic insects and that I needed more stuff.

When I tried to get my wife to relocate to better fly-fishing country, she told me she didn't want to leave her friends. When I found out it was just the one friend she didn't want to leave, I got the paperwork done and relocated. When I found myself a member of a sub-sub-subculture (collecting bamboo fly rods and exclusively dry-fly fishing), I realized that I *did* have a problem—I needed to make more money. I took a seasonal job, working six months out of the year so my summers could be devoted to fly-fishing. My winters were taken up with work, repairing rods, tying flies, and pouring over BLM maps looking for ways into places that I had yet to fish.

I became incapable of holding conversations for more than five minutes unless I was talking about fly-fishing. I watched as dinner date's eyes glaze over when I mentioned a new reel or a new fly pattern I'd come up with. I didn't want to talk about feelings. I wanted to talk about how a Phillipson taper was better in the wind than a Garrison taper. When I mentioned I'd just dropped three grand on a fly-rod, they'd get a look in their eyes that I'd seen before—on frightened cats. Relationships lasted until I heard, "Do you have to wear that funny looking hat everywhere we go?" I was incompatible with the opposite sex.

So I got a dog.

One day I was coming down the canyon after one of the best days of fishing I'd ever had, puffing on a (once forbidden) cigar, my Chesapeake Bay Retriever on the seat beside me, when it hit me. I was living the life I had read about in all those fly-fishing books. I had arrived—and it had only cost me one marriage, four relationships, and a lucrative career.

Kindred Spirits

I came west from the Southeast, where rivers are wide, muddy, and polluted. One river I fished was more cesspool than river, and it makes me cringe when I think of what must have been on my hands as I stripped my fly line through my fingers. Most bridges had a fisherman's access, a place to park, with a footpath leading down and along the bank. One day I approached one of these bridges with the intention of wetting a fly and saw the side with the easier access was occupied, and I'd be forced to take the side with the steeper path.

After stringing up my rod, I walked over to get a look at the steep, muddy trail. The path, more drop-off than path, terminated at some old bridge pillars sticking about two feet out of the mud. No sweat, I thought—it's funny how you can bullshit yourself when you want to get to a fishing hole. Looking over at the opposite bank, I caught sight of the other angler sitting on a bucket with his tackle box, bait can, and cooler within easy reach. His poles were propped up on forked sticks, and I counted three bobbers floating thirty feet in front of him. Bait fisherman, I registered. No problem, I thought. After all, he was a fellow fisherman, and thus a kindred spirit. I raised my hand in greeting, but my gesture of goodwill was ignored. No problem I thought, after all, there was plenty of river for both of us.

I'd made it halfway down before my feet shot from under me, and I remember looking up at my muddy boots outlined against Georgia pines as I went over the embankment and landed on one of the old pillars. I lay there, breath knocked out, white light flashing behind my eyes, making strange sucking sounds until I was finally able to sit up and pull up my shirt to check the damage. I had an oozing gash under my left breast that ran around my torso and disappeared from sight. I looked to the other bank thinking I would see my fellow angler showing signs of concern, perhaps even offering to come and give me a hand, but what I saw was him disappearing over the top of the hill with fish poles, cooler, and bucket. It wasn't until then I noticed my kindred spirit belonged to a demographic that nowadays prefers to be called little people.

Using the offending pillar, I pulled myself upright and slowly made my way back up the hill, gasping out Randy Newman's hit song "Short People" through clinched teeth.

I *have* met good people on the stream, developing friendships that lasted for decades … and some that only lasted for a day. I still fish with some of them, but some have passed on, and we now fish the waters of memory.

I had taken a job that put me in the middle of some of the best fly-fishing in the country. I had weekends off, so on Fridays after work I'd head for the river, set up camp, and fish until late Sunday evening. Fishing a big Western river was a new experience for me. And it blew my mind. I had no clue. I'd pound the river twelve hours and catch one or two fish. It was frustrating. I could see other fisherman hauling in one fish after another. I tried to learn from watching the more productive anglers, but it wasn't working. I was drowning in festering ignorance. The other fishermen were unfriendly and unwilling to ease my suffering by offering advice. After all, I was just another rube with out-of-state plates. My inexperience shined like a jewel in a goat's ass: my old fiberglass rod (everybody else was using graphite), my waders (more accurately, ditch boots), and my fishing vest (a pair of bib overalls) were clear signs I had not paid the initiation fee to be welcomed into their fraternity. But help was on the way in the form of a kindly old man named Ed Jones.

I met Ed one cold, foggy Sunday morning. He was sitting on the back of his jeep struggling with his waders when I walked up.

Looking me up and down he exclaimed, "Well goddamn!" It was a greeting I would hear many times over the years.

Ed was in his mid-sixties. His head had a thick crop of white hair, and his frame was bent from years of hard work. The joints of his hands were swollen from arthritis, and he had magnifiers clipped to his thick glasses so he could see to tie on flies. We made small talk as he rigged up. I told him I was from back East and would be working in the area for the next few months, and he told me he fished there, rain or shine, every Sunday. He said the river was his Church, and it was there on the river he felt closest to his Maker. I noticed he kept looking at my rod and was starting to feel a little self-conscious and about to be on my way, when he grabbed my rod and began rebuilding my leader, complete with flies from his box. As he worked on my leader, he explained what he was doing, and, more importantly, why. Satisfied he had me squared away, he handed me my rod and said, "Follow me." And I did.

That day under Ed's tutelage I went from catching one or two fish a day to catching four and five an hour. When we parted that evening he said, "I'll see you next Sunday." It was a fishing date that I kept for the next three months. A few years later, when I relocated to the area, we picked up where we'd left off.

Over the years Ed crippled with age and came to rely on *me*. I built *his* leaders, tied on *his* flies, and helped him with his waders. He'd lean on me as we moved up and down the river, his weight lighter with each passing year. We had gotten into the habit of calling each other during the week to talk fishing and make plans for the next Sunday, so one week when I hadn't heard from him by Friday I gave him a ring. I was surprised to hear a strange voice on the other end—it was Ed's son. He told me Ed had passed earlier in the week.

I haven't fished that river since that last Sunday we fished together. But I go there, to look, sit, and remember. When clouds slide down the mountains to hide the river in foggy mist, I almost see Ed casting—there … at the edge of sight—and hear his greeting, "Well goddamn!"

Two

The Life

Boom Box Saint

It was a special place, a place that had become an old friend, a friend you share things with—not a beer or a pinch of Copenhagen—inside things. For years I had the place to myself, so when I started running into other fisherman and campers, I was pissed and defensive. I wanted these people to get out of my face and go find their own special place. At first it was just one or two, and that wasn't so bad. They seemed like kindred spirits, looking for the same thing I was looking for, a place to go when you need to cleanse your soul, a place to hide from flatlanders and political bullshit, a place to take a friend who has a broken heart.

It was there I performed my yearly ritual of keeping a few Trout for dinner to stay in touch with the base reason for fishing in the first place, a practice that put me on the fringes of polite angling society, according to friends who considered taking trout murder and me no better than a North Georgia corn-soaker who follows hatchery trucks around until they dump his dinner into the crick. But I gave little thought to those friends as I rolled my trout in cornmeal, fried them in bacon grease, and washed them down with cool creek water liberally laced with Irish whiskey.

I shared one such meal with a doctor who was traveling cross-country to New York promoting a children's book he had illustrated. He gave me a signed copy, which I still have, and it's one of my prized possessions.

Then, somehow, word got out. Car loads of yuppies started showing up wearing ball caps sporting logos of high-end fishing gear. With their shiny, new gear, they looked down their polished yuppie noses at me in my ratty old slouch hat, fish and jelly stained vest, and patched waders. They hadn't been in the sport long enough to appreciate an antique bamboo rod and probably figured I was just some eccentric old fart, or worse, a bait fisherman. They had pretty women with them who wouldn't look you in the eye—as if ashamed of the company they were keeping—and dogs (always retrievers) that seemed starved for attention; one scratch behind the ear usually had them hanging out at my camp for the rest of the weekend—the dogs that is. Then the real bait fishermen showed up.

One afternoon a car with what appeared to be two whole families and some change pulled down the hill into camp. They jumped out and scattered like a flock of turkeys. The older children headed upstream shouting and throwing rocks in the water; the men headed down stream with their fish poles, six-packs, and bait buckets; and the women headed for the creek with their toddlers and began changing babies, throwing dirty diapers into the bushes, and shampooing their hair.

I decided to head down the creek to get away from them and do some fishing. As I passed the men, I noticed they were fishing with worms in a section of creek reserved for artificial flies and lures. Thinking they may not be familiar with the regulations, I stopped and explained to them they were in the wrong section and told them how to get to the bait fishing section. Later, on my way back to camp, I saw they were still there and still fishing with worms. And they had a stringer of fish clearly over the limit. I told them again they were fishing in the wrong place. One of them turned, sneered, and asked with a heavy Latin accent, "Are you the game warden?" I said, "No. I'm the son-of-a-bitch who's going to take down your license number and give it to the game warden." With that they packed up and left. After they left, I filled up a thirty gallon trash bag with the dirty diapers, pop cans, and toilet paper they'd left in their wake. Shortly after that, I made my last trip to my hideaway.

I set up camp one Friday night in my usual spot and was hoping to have the place to myself, but Saturday morning a group pulled in and set up camp right next to me. Everything seemed fine until the sun went down—then the party broke out. They cranked their boom box full blast and the drinking, shouting, and loud music went on until about four a.m. when they gradually drifted off to their tents to crash. I waited until I was sure they were good and passed out, quietly broke camp, and loaded my truck. When I was ready to pull out, I slipped into their camp, found the boom box, placed it on the trail in front of my truck, and ran over it on my way out.

I found a new place. The hike in is tough. But that's okay—flatlanders don't stray far from the road, and I usually have the place to myself.

Shattered Dreams

Every fly rod has a sweet spot, a smooth-flowing, singular rhythm; when you find it, it's poetry. With bamboo rods that sweet spot is pronounced and unique. That rhythm is the rod's personality—you don't just fish a bamboo rod, you commune with it. Bamboo feels alive when you have a fish on, and I love watching a rod work, its ripened color throbbing against the living green backdrop of a Ponderosa. I like to sit on a creek bank admiring the craftsmanship that goes into them and wondering what was going on in the maker's life as he planned the sections and wrapped the guides. I wonder if the original owner is still alive and where he fished, and I wonder what stories the rod would tell if it could talk.

I get attached to my rods and feel guilty when one gets neglected in favor of another. I've had some rods for over thirty years. They're like old friends, and I love them. But I don't baby them. I fish them hard. (One rod-maker claims that all my rods are combat tested). Other than adopting the wearing of protective underpants, there really is no way to prepare for the day when you break a favorite rod.

I don't shave my head, don sackcloth, and sprinkle ashes, but I feel like I should. It's like a heavy weight on your shoulders driving you to your knees. The guilt overwhelms ... because it's your fault. Who else's could it be? You look away, and back, hoping it will go away. You try to figure out how it happened, and when you do, you swear you'll never do that again. I'd fished with bamboo rods for over twenty-five years before I broke my first one.

It was a sweet little three-weight I'd found on consignment at a local fly shop. I've always been of the opinion that anything smaller than a four-weight rod is a waste of time, but the little rod was beautifully crafted. And the price was right.

THE LIFE

I hadn't fished the little rod in a while and was feeling guilty, so I was determined to fish it that day. When I got to the creek, the wind was gusting, and I thought about going with a heavier rod but blew it off. I tied on a bushy number twelve Adams without giving much thought to that either. I fished for a couple of hours, bucking a stiff head wind, and casting the bushy Adams was like waving a flag in a hurricane.

I was casting past a rocky point and didn't notice my fly line had gotten trapped in the rocks. I pulled up for a backcast and snapped the rod just below the ferrule. When I got home, I called the fly shop and got the contact information for the maker. He said he could fix the rod, and I ordered a couple of more rods from him that day. He told me that even though the reason the rod broke was the fly line getting hung up, I shouldn't have been trying to buck a strong headwind with a big bushy fly on the little rod. He told me the weakest point on a rod is just below the ferrule, and that is where most rods normally break. I told him to never, ever use the word normally when talking about breaking fly rods.

I recently shattered the tip on a wonderful three-piece six-weight. I spotted several risers at a bend pool and eased into position, intending to pick them off one by one. Of course, my first cast wrapped around a willow branch on the far side of the pool. The fish were still rising, so I gave the line a tug to see if it would come loose. It didn't. I was so pissed at myself for making a shitty cast that I gave the line a hard jerk—jerk can either be a verb or a noun, by the way—shattering the rod about four inches down from the tip. Not wanting to explain what I'd done to the rod, I tried making the repair myself. I wrapped the shatter with two layers of thread and then put ten coats of varnish over it. It fished, but I could tell it wouldn't last long; I'm having a new tip made for it now.

There are hundreds of ways to break fly rods: slamming them in car doors and tail gates, snagging them on bushes, and falling on them, to name a few. I've had some close calls falling down, but I've developed a technique that's a real rod saver. Instead of throwing my hands out in front of me to break my fall, I concentrate on tossing the rod clear of the area of operation, taking the impact on my chin. I got the idea while driving past a liquor store one day with my ex. A guy was just leaving the store with a brown paper bag cradled in his arms. He stumbled and fell, but had the presence of mind to tuck the bottle into his mid-section, covering it with both arms like a halfback fighting for a first down on third 'n' eight, taking the full impact to the curb on his face. My ex said, "We should go back and see if he needs help." "He's fine," I told her, "He didn't spill a drop."

How some breaks happen are mysteries that will never be solved. They just happen, like a big butt on a girlfriend. You're going along and everything's fine when you suddenly realize that something doesn't feel right. You look to see what's wrong—and there it is.

The Storm

I had the trailhead to myself as I strung my rod and prepared to head out. I remember staring at the poncho rolled up behind the seat of the truck. I find those times when you stare at something and your mind goes blank to be harbingers of trouble; I once went blank staring at a miniskirt and wound up married to it. But the robin-egg-blue sky was clear, and the trail down the creek was rough—more game trail than footpath—and anything I could do to lighten my load would be to my advantage, so I gave the poncho no more thought.

The little tailwater left the small reservoir, meandering a couple of hundred yards across a meadow before dropping into a narrow canyon. I'd fished there before, but had only made it down the creek a couple of miles to where the trail spiderwebbed, sometimes wandering up the steep slope to disappear over the ridge, and sometimes ending abruptly on the precipitous hillside, leaving you ledged-up with no option but to slide back down to the creek on your ass. The overgrazed hillsides are sparsely covered in blue sage, Scotch thistle, and tufts of crested wheat grass. Much of the creek is lined on both sides by sheer outcrops that in several places stretch across the creek to form a series of small four- and five-foot waterfalls, each with plunge pools holding fifteen- to eighteen-inch cutthroats. I took the risky game-trail detours around the deep pools to keep from spooking the fish, crisscrossing the creek several times on the way in without giving much thought to the return trip. I'd be fishing and wading my way back, and the little waterfalls were climbable.

When I'd made it in about twice as far as I had previously, I sat down to rest for a few minutes before starting to fish. The several ninety-degree turns the creek took and the steep canyon walls blocked my view of the horizon, so when I noticed a bank of cottony clouds peeking over the ridge, they were already close. Weather changes quickly in the mountains, sometimes so quickly your ears pop. I knew that, but fluffy, white clouds don't look threatening, and if it did rain, the chances were it wouldn't last long and would blow on by.

I took off fishing and was having a good day catching a few nice cutts at each hole. I'd been fishing a couple of hours before I thought to check the sky again. I could still see the white clouds, but now there was a lower layer of disorganized cadet-gray clouds. I knew I should pick up the pace and start thinking about getting out of there, but every pool I came to had trout rising, and I couldn't pass up casting to them.

When a gust of cold wind caused me to look up at the rim of the canyon, the fluffy clouds were gone. The wispy, gray clouds were on top of me; and a third layer of densely packed, gunmetal-blue clouds was rolling in fast and low—with purpose. Deep, distant thunder grumbled, and puffs of dust sprang up on the hillsides where raindrops big as horse turds began to fall. I had a clear mental picture of the rolled poncho nestled snugly behind the seat of the truck.

I reeled in and started up the creek as fast as I could waddle in my waders. An ear splitting crack just above and behind me caused me to crouch down on the balls of my feet. I could smell burning ozone and feel electricity in my hair. That's when the bottom fell out; in an instant I was soaked through to the skin.

The felt soles on my waders caked up with mud, leaving me no traction on the muddy trail. I squatted on the bank for a few minutes hoping the storm would blow over, but it settled in on top of me. Rivulets of water ran down the hillsides turning them to mud, and the creek rose dramatically and turned the color of the khaki slopes. I couldn't see to wade around the deep pools, and my mud caked waders made scaling the now mud-slimed, rocky falls impossible. The only place I could get traction was in the thick stands of willow. I took shelter under a rocky overhang until the spouts of water rushing down either side of it made me realize it could wash loose and come down on top of me. The wind picked up, the temperature dropped, and I sat shivering in my wet clothes. The wind blew up and then down the canyon, changing directions instantly, and at one point the rain turned to sleet, blasting and stinging my face and hands. I needed to get back to the truck before the sun went down. Dying of hypothermia was now a stark reality. I did have three ways to start a fire with me in my survival pack, but there was no way to get a fire started in this downpour.

I tried moonwalking along the trail, but after taking a couple of hard falls, I kept to the thick willows. When I came to the end of one stand of willows, I'd crawl on my hands and knees to the next stand. My glasses fogged and made the going even harder, as I couldn't tell where I was in the canyon, or how far I had left to go.

I finally reached a spot in the canyon where I knew there was a four-wheeler trail about a hundred yards up the slope. I would have to crawl up the hill, but the trail would dump me out on a good gravel road about a mile from the truck. I tossed my rod ahead of me and crawled to it using sage and tufts of wheat grass to pull my way up. When I topped the ridge on my hands and knees, I found I was able to stand and move along the trail as long as I stayed in the middle between the muddy ruts. I got to the truck covered in mud, soaked to the skin, and shivering from the cold just as the skylight faded.

I take a ziplock bag of dryer lint soaked in white gas with me now (you can start a fire under the most extreme conditions with that), and I've got cleated waders I keep rolled up behind the seat … next to the poncho.

Back In The Saddle

I turned onto the dirt road trying to remember the directions I'd been given—take the right fork, take the left fork, cross the bridge, pass the sheep camp … and something else.

The sheep camp didn't surprise me—this being sheep country—but using one for a landmark seemed dodgy; I was pretty sure sheep camps moved with the herd. I was wishing I'd written the directions down when I spotted the sheep camp coming up on the right. Two sheepherders had a horse on its back with its legs sticking straight up in the air. One herder was holding the horse down, while the other was attempting to shoe the horse. All participants looked distressed, and all were sweating profusely ... I mentally checked off sheep camp.

The road looked good, but I knew that could change and it could become nothing more than a glorified game trail just around the next bend. Adding to the pucker factor, I was dragging a horse trailer, and my horse, Red, was bouncing back and forth threatening to throw us off the road.

I was to meet up with my friend Cody for some camping and fishing. Cody was a cowboy; not the boot-scootin', feather-in-hat, Nashville kind, but the bull strong, hog ugly, snuff dippin', bulldog-a-wild-horse-and-never-spit kind. Cody belongs to a subculture of fly-fishers that consider the horse a requisite accoutrement to the sport.

Cody and his brothers sold horses and took great pride in their ability to match horse to rider. They had "experienced horses for inexperienced riders, inexperienced horses for experienced riders, and for people who don't like to ride ... they had horses that don't like to be rode." It had taken Cody most of the winter to convince me that in order to get into the really good fishing I needed a horse—and I needed to buy that horse from him.

I finally found his camp: an old truck, horse trailer, and tent situated in front of a huge fire pit. Although it was noon on a hot day in July, Cody was standing by the fire drinking a beer. I have noticed that no matter how hot it is, if you build a fire, people *will* stand around it, an oddity that probably dates back to the dawn of time deserving further study. I hobbled Red, set up my tent, and moseyed over to stand by the fire.

After some small talk, we decided to saddle up and ride over to the creek and do some fishing.

I followed Cody up a trail that soon led onto a narrow ledge overlooking a 100-foot drop. I was relieved when the trail took a hard right and headed up the slope away from the ledge, but just as I made the turn, Cody's horse shied at something, spooking Red, who took off going backward as hard as he could for the edge of the cliff. I jumped off and got him stopped just before he stepped off into the abyss. I walked Red up the slope until we were what I considered a safe distance from the drop-off before remounting.

When I caught up to him, Cody was waiting for me in front of a pile of deadfall, leaning on his saddle horn, looking bored. He said, "Why you walkin' that horse? If God would've wanted man to walk, he'd've give him four legs."

Beyond the pile of deadfall lay a meadow that sloped down to a thick stand of willows. I heard the creek gurgling below.

Cody eased his horse through the deadfall with me right behind. I had almost made it through when Red made four long jumps into the meadow and started bucking. He bucked a couple of times, then set up into a spin, slinging me out of the saddle. I landed hard, but managed to keep hold of the reins, which I thought a huge accomplishment, considering. I looked over at Cody for some sign of approval, but he just leaned forward on his saddle horn and looked bored. I knew the "cowboy way" demanded I get right back on, and as I put my foot in the stirrup I asked Cody, "How'd I look?" To which he replied, "Good … for the first couple of jumps." I climbed back aboard, and as quick as my butt hit the saddle Red went into another spin, flinging me out of the saddle again. As I was about to mount up again, I noticed a dead tree limb stuck under Red's back cinch. I pulled the limb out and was tightening the cinch when Cody said, "We ain't goin' to get much fishin' in if you and Red don't quit messin' around."

"We're good now," I told him, and we headed on into the creek bottom.

We crossed the creek to an island where we hobbled the horses, strung our rods, and took off up the creek, casting to pocket water.

We'd caught five or six trout apiece when we hit an open flat where two creeks came together. After agreeing on a time to meet back at the horses, we split up, Cody taking the right fork, me the left.

Fishing alone in bear country can be a little spooky. It's something you have to get your head around, but I decided long ago I'd rather get eaten by a bear than lay around dying of some terrible disease. Besides, on this trip, if anything got eaten it would be the horses. And after the crap Red had been pulling, I was down with it.

I'd managed to cover a lot of ground when I realized I would have to hustle to get back to the horses by the appointed time. When I got back to the horses, Cody wasn't there, and it was only after I had my gear packed that he showed up saying we needed to reach the main trail before it got dark.

We were mounted and had begun to move off when Red took three giant leaps forward, landing us in the middle of the stream. I looked over at Cody, who was leaning on his saddle horn, looking bored, and said, "I think this bastard wants to buck again." "Just take the hobbles off," he told me. I dismounted into two-foot of water, which filled my boots, and groped around until I got the hobbles unbuckled.

It was now pitch black, and we crisscrossed up the slope searching for, but not finding the trail. At the top of the hill, Cody took off with such an air of confidence that I asked him if he'd found the trail. He said, "Yeah … but not yet." We finally reached what looked like a meadow, and as we started across Cody told me to watch out for old down fencing and piles of barbed wire that might be laying around.

Cody had just hollered back that he'd found the trail when I heard the ping of wire. I pulled Red up, dismounted, and began running my hands down his legs to see if we were tangled in barbed wire. Feeling around in the darkness, I found both of Red's hind legs were standing in a coil of wire, and after much cursing and fumbling, I was finally able to free us.

As we made our way back to camp we passed several campfires, but Cody said we should give them a wide berth, as the firelight would ruin the horses' night vision. I didn't know horses had night vision, but was glad to hear it. Armed with that information, I assumed Red had stepped into the coil of wire for the hell of it. Clearly, Red had been out to *get me* from the *get-go*.

When we got back to camp, we cared for the horses and Cody sat me down by the fire, handed me a beer, and began giving me some much needed instruction in horsemanship.

Beaver Slapped

According to Michigan state law, beaver dams cannot be built or maintained except by beavers. I find this fascinating, as I've often wondered if by consuming grubs, berries, roots, rodents, and backpackers I'd be able to produce bear scat, but there's probably a law against that, as well.

In the past, the Department of Natural Resources would blow up problem beaver dams with dynamite, and I often find pieces of detonation cord at old dam sites; however, lately they have taken to placing large rocks along the tops of beaver dams in an effort to adjust the flow of water going over them without removing or otherwise damaging the dam. I wonder if this policy of placing rocks on dams extends their natural life and interferes with spawning fish. Beaver dams get washed out during spring runoff, which is natural and good. And for the fish moving into these drainages from lakes and reservoirs to spawn, the damage done during runoff is essential, as it allows the trout to move freely up the creeks to prime spawning beds.

In places overpopulated with beaver, trout get trapped in small beaver ponds, and I often catch deformed fish with large heads and long, snaky bodies in these ponds. On their own, beaver will periodically relocate dams as they exhaust the supply of the tender willows and aspens they love, forming ponds throughout the whole drainage, changing the course of the stream, and creating fresh habitat for their riparian neighbors.

Fishing a beaver pond upstream is tough. The commotion caused when the fly-line hits the static water of the pond spooks the fish, and your fly line always gets tangled in the sticks and limbs of the dam. You can get around spooking the fish by using a long leader and delicate cast, but I have found fishing beaver ponds from above more productive. I let the fly drift down until the fly line straightens out and then give it a few twitches. This method works extremely well with nymphs. After the nymph settles to the bottom, I begin giving the fly movement by slowly stripping the line. I frequently stand in one spot and pick off five or six trout using this technique.

I often come across beaver slides (places where the beaver enter and exit the stream) that are big enough to resemble the mouth of a small feeder creek. I don't know if these large slides are made by large beaver or if they're the result of repeated use by small beaver, but they're big enough to give me the willies. They get me thinking about the tall tales I've heard of people being attacked by rabid beavers. I always stop and peer up the slide into the shadowy willows half expecting to see a giant beaver sitting there drooling and giggling and quivering with disease, waiting to pounce.

I've gotten close to beaver in the purple shades of evening with neither me nor the beaver being aware of the other's presence—until the last minute.

Late one afternoon, I headed downstream from camp to fish a stretch of creek located between two large beaver ponds. I found a shallow riffle marked by several rocks sticking halfway out of the water where I could cross the creek and approach a particularly productive bend pool from below. The fishing was good, and I'd caught eight or ten fish when I realized I'd stayed too long and would have to hustle in order to get back to camp before dark. In the twilight, I could just make out the rocks that marked the crossing. I'd made it to the middle of the stream when one of the rocks I'd just stepped over slapped the water with its tail and shot upstream between my legs. I came down on dry land on the other side of the creek, managing a standing broad jump that would've easily qualified me for Olympic competition. (I've since taken to bringing fresh pants on camping trips for emerge-ncies.) I got my breath back, finished marking my trail, and headed back to camp … thankful that I hadn't been wearing chest waders.

The Fall Of Man

There *is* one certainty in fly-fishing: you *will* fall down. I'm not talking about slips, stumbles, and trips that do little harm except to the ego. I'm talking about the kinds of falls that shatter fly rods, knees, and whisky bottles.

When evaluating the degree of difficulty of a fall and explaining ripped waders, torn hands, shattered fly rods, noticeable limps, and soiled pants to friends and significant others, proper nomenclature is helpful. There's the sprawl, nosedive, header, plummet, topple, and the ever entertaining moonwalk.

A sprawl is performed by pitching forward, leaving your feet behind, throwing your arms out to the side, and landing on your chest or face before your knees touch the ground.

A nosedive is any fall where impact is taken above the upper lip.

A header (similar in form to the nosedive) involves a head-over-heels tuck 'n' roll with the initial impact taken anywhere above the shoulders. When preformed on a steep slope, the header can be done repeatedly, gaining momentum with each roll until forward motion is arrested or deflected by a rock or a tree.

A plummet (my personal favorite because of the opportunity it affords for spectacle) must be initiated from a height of at least four feet—point of impact, optional.

Gravity is of course the root cause of all falls and is best illustrated by a fall I call the topple: You're busting through a stand of willows when you get off balance and just topple over, embracing gravity without a struggle—normally landing in a thorn bush. I recently did a topple that had me preforming pocketknife surgery on my hands for a week.

Gravity, mud, and felt-bottom waders combine to produce some spectacular falls. I first became aware of this while contemplating my mud-caked boots outlined against a clear blue sky as I went over a fifteen-foot embankment. Luckily, I was able to break the fall by landing on a sixteen-inch diameter post that was sticking two-feet out of the mud. When I was able to breathe again and inspect the damage, I had a two-inch wide gash that ran from just under my left breast to the center of my back. Muddy waders are excellent for preforming the maneuver I call the moonwalk, as well.

Unlike the popular dance move that propels you backward, this moonwalk propels you forward, while you peddle backward as rapidly as you can. I once watched a friend of mine do the moonwalk for twenty-feet until he was waist deep in the Chattahoochee River. I did a version of the moonwalk on scree once. (Scree: an accumulation of loose stones or rocky debris lying on a slope or at the base of a hill or cliff most useful in allowing dumbass to come full circle.) My feet eventually shot out from under me and I went sledding and turtling on my back for thirty-feet and over a ten-foot cut bank, landing in the river on my butt. The moonwalk can also be done standing in place while gradually picking up tempo until you tire and just sit down. (This seems to be a particular favorite among spectators.)

Unless the good fishing is on the other side, or you are in a hurry to get to the bottom of the hill, slopes strewn with scree should be avoided; however, muddy or scree-strewn slopes can—in a pinch—be tested for stability by graciously allowing your fishing partner to go first. While form is important, proper falling etiquette must be observed at all times, as well.

All falls must be performed in silence. Unmanly shrieks, screams, and little girl noises diminish any respect gained by the degree of difficulty of the fall; however, an audible "oomph" upon impact *is* permissible and lets onlookers know you've survived the fall. And, from the reactions of all *my* friends, apparently adds comedic relief.

No fall is complete without proper follow-through. Always assume there are spectators and remember that it's how you fall that matters, and do it with style. Staunch the bleeding—this is real he-man stuff—by packing the wounds with mud, then move off in a composed manner. Once you're confident there are *no* witnesses and nobody will hear your whimpers, curl into the fetal position and wait for the pain to subside.

A couple of years ago, I took a fall that had me limping for most of the summer. I'd spotted some rising trout holding behind a large rock on the other side of the river. Halfway across, I was watching the rises and planning my cast when my feet shot out from under me and I came down hard on a sharp rock with my knee. (Knee: the part of the body most useful in locating sharp objects.) White pain shot through my brain, pain that causes blinding flashes of light to flicker behind your eyes and makes you sick to your stomach, pain that causes you to question your ability to make it back to the truck and makes you wonder how long it will be before they find your body. I stayed on hands and knees sucking air in short breaths through clenched teeth, waiting for the pain to subside. I thought about a friend who'd just gone under the knife for a knee replacement and wondered if I, too, would be getting fitted for a new skid. I pulled my good leg under me and stood up, testing the injured leg by slowly putting weight on it until satisfied I could walk. I was digging around in my waders for my first-aid kit—a pint of medicinal whisky—when I felt something warm and wet trickling down my leg. I prayed it was blood.

SKUNKED

I've *caught* twenty-four inch cutts on gossamer tippet with a four-weight bamboo rod. I've pounded 'em up to my hand-tied dries when there wasn't a fish rising for a hundred miles. I've fished big rivers and high-country headwaters and had fifty-fish days. I've crossed swollen creeks without bridges, dodged summer lightning, been trapped by late spring snows ... I don't have anything left to prove.

Anyway, that's the kind of smoke I was blowing the other day when Appleton called to get a fishing report.

"That bad huh?"

"I couldn't get a rise if I doped my fly with Stink Bait ... I even thought about tying on a dropper," I whispered.

"Whoa! Don't do anything you'll regret."

"Look," I said, "maybe we've gotten too hung up on the catching. I mean, fly-fishing should be about the inner man, not how big or how many fish we catch. It should be about communing with a well-crafted fly rod, finding the rhythm and poetry in a delicate cast, letting the beauty of the mountains and the sounds of the stream cleanse your soul ... You know, rediscovery ... getting back to nature? ... You still there?"

"... Who *else* you been talking to?"

"Nobody."

"Good. Call me when the fishing picks up."

Appleton was one of the first to go barbless. He became unpopular with the river guides when he tried to get the local fly shop to sell only barbless hooks. I've even known him to break the hook off and fish with an impotent fly when he got tired of catching fish, but he's caught up in the corporate rat race now; it's hard to get him out if the fish aren't biting.

I often get skunked when we fish together. I usually have the place scouted and let him take the lead as we head upstream, so the fish are spooked by the time I come along. Sometimes I catch up to him sitting at a nice-looking bend pool he's saved for me. He'll point his rod at the hole and say, "Let's get the skunks out of the boat." I don't think he really wants me to catch fish. I think he just doesn't want to be seen with a guy who isn't catching fish.

After Appleton hung up, I realized the danger I'd put myself in. Word would get around that I'd zened out, shaved my head, and was wandering the backcountry wearing a loincloth and sprinkling ashes. My solitary lifestyle with its ensuing lack of what—for propriety's sake—we'll call female companionship would be blamed for my deteriorating mental state and moral decline. There would be meetings; I'd get voted off the island—or worse. (The last time my friends thought I'd spun out they'd tried fixing me up—it was love at 425 pounds.)

The next day I had a twenty fish day and was able to abandon my new religion and resume wearing pants.

It's in early spring between the first warm days and the big runoff that I usually get skunked. The creeks are running high and off color, and the trout are hugging the bottoms of deep pools in a state of suspended animation. You can catch them if you bump them on the nose with a Copper John or a Pheasant's Tail, but I'm stubborn about using dries. I'd figured that since I was already a fly fisherman (the most hated demographic among fishermen), the next logical step was to become a dry-fly purist (the most hated demographic among fly fishers). And being an old white guy (the most hated demographic on the planet), I made the transition smoothly.

In my fly-fishing infancy, I'd become frantic when getting skunked, my level of panic directly in proportion to the amount of money spent on fishing gear. I had the best in sporting equipment and still wasn't catching fish. I looked marvelous, but I obviously needed better gear.

Back when my skill level didn't match my equipment, I'd fish for twelve hours at a stretch without seeing a rise. I once fished like that for three days in a downpour, stopping for short breaks to crawl into my tent—where I poured. On the afternoon of the third day, I found myself standing in the middle of a muddy creek, nose running, holding a bleached-out, six-inch German-Brown in pruned fingers, thinking what miserable specimens we both were of our respective species.

Nowadays, early spring fishing really *is* more about getting into the mountains, shaking off shack fever, and picking out the wind knots that formed in my head over the winter. When you hike for an hour to get to a stream and find it running high and muddy, you can turn around and hike back out, or find a good sittin' log and enjoy the view. I know I can tie on a nymph and catch fish, but that's not what I'd seen myself doing all winter. I look around more and wonder at what I missed when I was squinting at an aquarium net and pawing through my fly box for answers; besides, I can always come back and try again tomorrow. Most people can't do that. I remember that sense of urgency, being limited to a Saturday now and then, or one week in the summer.

I've never been a lip ripping, don't-make-me-take-my-pants-down trophy-trout-hunter. I'm satisfied with my little high-country cutts, so on fishless early-spring days, I'm content to just go through the motions and get the kinks out of my cast, watch young stoneflies crawl up my waders and only think about changing from an Adams, be happy to be alive and still able to make the hike in. In a few days the streams will run clear and the fishing will be as good as ever, so it's not bad sitting in the sun, warming the knotted muscles in my shoulders, and thinking about the good day I'm having doing no harm ... Not bad at all.

Spring Crossing

I stood looking at the snowfields above me with a bad feeling in my gut. Where the swollen creek cut its way through, the snow was four-foot deep; I'd never get through. I'd just get wet if I tried, and staying dry was a priority now. Technically it was spring, but a guy could still get toe tagged winter kill up here. On the slope leading up to the snow-banked ridge above me, water gushed from every rat hole. The whole mountain was a sieve. I looked back at the tree line from which I had emerged and started thinking about gathering wood for a fire and spending the night. I could split a power bar with my dog, Touch, bank up a fire, and wait until the wee hours when the runoff froze. We could cross the creek then, when it would be at its lowest. But we'd still have a five mile hike to get back to the truck—and we'd be wet. I'd screwed up. Ignoring the deep snow on the ridges above me, I'd entered an area bordered by water on all sides during the spring melt.

The thermometer had read twenty-nine degrees that morning as I drove up the canyon. It was the time of the year when one side of the road showed the green-up of spring, while the other side was a scene from a Christmas card, with snow still hanging in the trees and covering the ground. I had stepped across the little creek that morning.

We'd hiked to the back side of the reservoir, me casting to the edge of the ice, Touch swimming out to the splashes of my Wooly Bugger. The day turned gorgeous and warm. I started thinking I'd overdressed.

At noon, I hiked up a slope and found a log in a little meadow where I sat and ate my peanut butter sandwich. I gave Touch a dog biscuit, and we stretched out in the sun and took a nap.

Long before we got back to the creek we'd crossed that morning, I heard it. The little creek was now the color of latte and raging out of its banks. Where I'd stepped across that morning, it was now twenty-yards wide and chest deep. A rush of adrenalin hit me. And I was ashamed I knew the *color* of latte. My only chance to get out of there before nightfall was to head upstream and hope I could find a place to cross. It would be a steep climb, and if I couldn't find a place to cross, I'd wind up spending the night. I started thinking I'd underdressed.

I had a survival kit with me—first-aid kit, a couple of power bars, bullion, instant coffee, and a bag of dryer lint with a couple of ways to get a fire started. I had one of those old army canteens with the metal cup I could boil water in. As long as I stayed dry I'd be ok. I took my jacket off and tied it around my waist to keep from sweating and started the climb. We headed up the creek looking for a spot to cross until we were above the timberline and found our way blocked by deep snow.

On the way up I'd spotted a pine tree that had washed into the creek and gotten wedged between two high cut banks. That down pine would be my best chance to get across. I still had two hours of daylight to make something happen. As I headed back to the down tree, I began working out a plan.

I figured I could cross on the upstream side of the tree by bracing against it and inching my way along. I'd use my jacket to make a bundle for the stuff I didn't want to get wet, and if I got to the middle of the creek, I'd throw the bundle on across so I'd have both hands free to finish the crossing and get up the steep bank. Once I got wet and had thrown the bundle over, I'd be committed to crossing; I wouldn't survive the night wet without a fire. I had one problem: The banks were too steep there for Touch to climb. Touch is a Chesapeake Bay Retriever and she'd rather swim than walk, so I wasn't worried about her getting across, I just needed to find a place where she could climb out. It would have to be close to the tree so I could start across quickly or she would try to get back to me. Getting her to cross without me wasn't a problem. I could throw anything over and she'd go after it.

I took my rod down, tied it into the bundle, and prayed that if I perished in the crossing, whoever found my high-dollar bamboo fly-rod wouldn't be a bait fisherman. Leaving the bundle at the down pine, I walked upstream until I found a place to send Touch over. I took my shoulder bag and slung it across, and Touch jumped in and started after it. I hotfooted it back to the tree, grabbed my bundle, and slid down the bank next to the tree into waist deep water. The icy water took my breath and slammed me against the tree. I could feel the gravel washing away under my feet and started thinking that maybe this wasn't such a good idea. If I lost my footing, I'd be swept under and held down by the tree and drowned. But I had to go with it now. If Touch saw me retreat, she would jump in to get back to me and *she* would be swept under the tree. We would both drown then, as I would go in after her. That would be an automatic reaction. I mean, it's not like rescuing a spouse, significant other, or fishing buddy, where you have time to assess the risk and go find a rope—she's my dog.

The water was chest deep in the middle of the creek, and I only stopped long enough to sling my bundle on over. After my hands were free, I made it the rest of the way across and clawed my way up the bank. I was covered in mud and soaked from the chest down.

The temperature would drop as soon as the sun went behind the mountain; I figured we had about an hour of daylight left. We were still four miles from the truck, but we could make good time by jogging and power walking. I poured the water out of my boots, gathered up my gear, and headed down the mountain. About half way back to the truck my feet started to hurt—wet socks and slip-on ditch boots suck for hiking. I managed to make it back just as the sun went down. The temperature had already dropped thirty degrees. My pants were froze stiff, and when I pulled my boots off, I had blisters the size of silver dollars on both feet. I started the truck and sat with my head on the steering wheel waiting for the heater to warm the cab. I looked over at Touch and said, "We got lucky this time girl."

The Survivor

There wasn't another angler in the canyon that day, and had I known how close the fire was and how fast it was moving, I wouldn't have been there either. I know I was the last one in there before the fire moved through, as I had to pass through a roadblock on my way out that night, and they weren't letting anybody else in. I got some strange looks from the forest rangers that morning as I was stringing up my rod, but one of them had assured me the night before the main canyon was in no danger.

The fishing that day was fantastic. I wouldn't have pestered those trout had I known they only had hours to live—had I known they would slowly suffocate from the ash and silt that turned that clear mountain stream the color of chocolate milk. At noon, I sat on the bank and ate my PB&J sandwich as ash from the fire fell around me and the sting of wood smoke made my nose run. It was the eerie orange hue the canyon took on and the spooky silence that finally made me pack it in and head for my truck. It took another seven days for the fire to burn through.

The devastation came later, when subsequent rainstorms sent flash floods and debris flows raging down the burned-out side-canyons, blowing out the road, silting the creek, and killing the fish. The logs and boulders that washed down the mountain—coupled with the human efforts to keep the road open—changed the course of that creek forever. I doubt if I could even find the spot where I ate my sandwich now. When I called the Utah State Biologist, he told me it would take decades for the stream to recover, and it wouldn't happen in *my* lifetime.

The fire had started from a lightning strike on the left fork and had moved down the creek and into the main canyon, leaving the upper section untouched. About a month after the main canyon burned, I hiked a couple of miles into the headwaters and fished my way back out without seeing the first sign of a fish. The bottom of the creek was coated in ash about a quarter-inch thick—the fish had suffocated.

I thought about that creek all winter, so as soon as the snow came off, I hiked in to see if the spring runoff had flushed the ash out. The stream was running clear and the coating of ash *was* gone, but there still wasn't a sign of life in the water.

I had given up on finding any fish and was walking along absentmindedly dapping my fly ahead of me when I got a rise to my Adams at a deep bend pool. I got a good look at the trout and figured it to be around eighteen-inches long. The biologist told me there were no plans to restock the drainage until the ground cover came back enough to stop the mudslides and debris flows from choking off the stream, so I knew the fish was a holdover from before the fire, a survivor.

That summer the area was hit hard by drought, and the stream became a trickling ghost of itself. I hiked in there four more times that summer without seeing another fish. I couldn't see how the big fish would survive the low, warm water, let alone the meat fishermen that descend on the high country to clean out the pools when the water gets low; after all, this is Utah, by God, where the people had been told by a "prophet" of God to profit by the land and they goddamn well do.

That next winter I spent a lot of time wondering if the big trout had died. I figured either some worm soaker or the drought conditions had finished the big guy off, but I wanted to find out, so as soon as the trail opened that spring I hiked straight to the bend pool where I had last seen the big fish.

I broke the hook off a #16 Adams; I just wanted to say "hi" without adding to the big guy's problems had he somehow managed to survive. I was startled when I got a rise on my first cast. Wanting to be sure it was the same fish, I spent some time casting different flies and watching the rises until I was satisfied it was him. On one of the rises, I clearly saw the bright red slash under its gills and I laughed out loud, delighted it was a native cutthroat. I fished the creek for a couple of miles above and below the pool without seeing another fish. After that, I started leaving my fly-rod back at the truck.

That summer I realized fly-fishing was just an excuse. It wasn't the fishing for wild trout that kept me coming back, it was the place itself—the way the shadows made it seem like every day was Saturday, the sounds of the creek probing through the narrow canyon, and the wind whispering in the quakies. It was the anticipation in the cumulous clouds that formed strong shapes and peeked over the rim of the wounded canyon. All too often that summer those clouds quickly massed, turned from fluffy white to gunmetal blue, thundered, flashed, and dumped a deadly deluge onto the burn-scar, sending walls of water and debris down the canyon that left boulders the size of cars and mud six-foot deep on the main road. Heavy equipment was brought in to clear and repair the washed-out road, and D-9 Cats were left sitting overnight in the middle of the creek, leaking oil and hydraulic fluid. What was once a blue-ribbon, wild-trout fishery became the saddest thing I'd ever seen.

The ease with which that ancient canyon had been destroyed scared me, and I felt small. The pursuit of wild trout that first drew me to the high country seemed insignificant. The shadows and sounds of the canyon and the drama of the clouds had always been there, but I hadn't noticed. They were new to me now—and fragile. All these years I'd missed something, and now some of it was gone, but the big cutt had somehow survived, and in that I found hope.

I hiked in several more times that summer with my dog, Touch, to check the stream conditions. I saw a few guys fishing, but they never stayed long. Then one day Touch and I were taking a break on our way out when this guy and his young son came up the trail. I asked how the fishing had been and the boy proudly showed me the big cutthroat he had strung on a willow branch. As he held it up for me to see his dad beamed, "It's his first fish on a fly rod, and he caught it all by himself."

"Yeah, and it was the only fish we seen all day," the boy added, grinning from ear to ear.

I grinned back and said, "That *is* a nice fish."

The Donner Party

When I topped out, iron-gray clouds lay heavy and full along the southern horizon—and south was where I wanted to go.

I pulled into a turnout and watched the storm advancing up the valley, shutting off light, shuttering the outside world. Without sun dazzling the fall colors, the mountains turned black, brown, and earthy as the storm moved in and squatted. Gossamer clouds hung in the saddles and then rolled down the slopes until the mountains vanished. Rain curtains formed a gray wall that extended across the southern end of the valley. Beads of water formed on the windshield, grew fat, slid down, and cut paths through misty film. Windows fogged, and I sat in blurred isolation listening to the rain tap, tap, tap the roof of the truck, drumming out any chance that I would get in some fishing that day. I wiped a hole in the window fog and watched a dense, gray sky turn gunmetal blue and slowly expand across the valley. The rain went from hard to steady, a steady that means it's settled in. This wasn't your normal quick-moving, high-country storm. It had a forty-day-forty-night feel to it. I decided to cut my losses and head for the top of the canyon and home.

Three years before, a wildfire raged through the canyon, and although much of the ground cover had returned, it remained badly burn-scarred and vulnerable to flooding. The gate used by the Forest Service to close the canyon road was open, but dropping into the canyon that day was like driving into a tunnel. Heavy clouds hung low, shrouding the canyon rim, and water cascaded down the canyon walls, forming creeks where there shouldn't be any. As I got farther into the canyon, rivulets of water became spouts of red, gravely mud, and each time I passed one of these falls, I wondered if I was lucky to make it through or if I should turn around and get the hell out of there. A group of cars passed me heading back up the canyon, and I soon found out why.

About halfway down I came to a washout. Large boulders, logs, and a layer of mud about a foot deep blocked the road. I had four-wheel drive and thought I might be able to move a log or two and a couple of the smaller boulders and pick my way through, but I decided to turn around and follow the group I'd seen heading up the canyon. I rounded a bend and spotted the group of cars circled up like a wagon train. They waved me down, so I pulled over and rolled down my window to see what was up.

One of the guys came over and said, "Hughes Canyon's blown out."

"North Hughes or South Hughes?"

"North."

"No way through?"

"No. Mud's three-foot deep, with lots of logs and boulders—have you got any food?"

I thought it a bit early in the ordeal to be worried about food, so I asked, "Is there a medical emergency?"

"No. It just looks like we'll be here a while," he replied.

I had some power bars and a couple of packs of cheese crackers ... so I told him no.

Then I noticed the men were all wearing black pants, white shirts, and black ties, and the women were wearing prairie dresses and blue and white ribbons in their hair. Fundamentalists—clannish, self-righteous, possibly even dangerous. I was a Gentile; thus, a prime candidate to be sacrificed for the greater good. Images of the Donner party flashed in my head, and I figured my best chance for survival was to get away from these good people, head back down the canyon, and see if I could pick my way through ... *before* they started drawing lots.

I got back to the washout, moved a couple of logs and oil-pan-crushing rocks, put the truck in four-wheel drive, and weaved my way through. I was thinking I'd tell the state bulls about the Donners once I cleared the canyon and could get cell service, when I came to another washout. This one was much bigger; there was no way to get through. In the distance, I could see two more washouts and a guy standing by a truck in the middle of the road at the last one. I waved to him and he waved back. Another truck pulled up, turned around, and headed back—going for help, I hoped.

I thought about making my way back to the Donners, but I figured they were probably already barbecuing children, so I stayed put, waiting for help to arrive.

The rain started up again much harder than before, so I backed to the top of a hill to get clear of the washout. At the mouth of the canyon, clouds layered in increasingly darker shades of gray moved in low, hiding the ridges, adding to my feeling of isolation.

Thunder rumbled, and lightning cracked somewhere on the ridge above me. I was looking up the washed-out side canyon when a red wall of water came churning around a bend, smashing and undercutting the outside wall before swinging back to the center of the canyon floor. Unseen boulders rumbled as the wall of muddy water surged through the little canyon picking up everything in its path. Chunks of canyon wall sloughed into the torrent and bushes and logs rode its crest. I'm not sure if I felt the ground shake, or if it was the roaring-locomotive sound that I felt. I watched pine trees fold into the thick, red pudding and car-size boulders roll into the road.

Fear produced by raging nature is different from any fear I've known. The terrifyingly unavoidable; relentlessly methodical; unimaginably swift power was paralyzing.

Columns of rain now appeared between me and the mouth of the canyon. Thunder crashed, skeletal fingers of lightning stabbed down in all directions, and the air smelled of burning ozone. Logs, trees, and thundering boulders came brawling out of another side canyon behind me, and I was now trapped on my little high spot in the road.

Finally, I spotted the flashing yellow lights of a front-end loader worming its way through the logs and boulders as it cut a path toward me. I warned the operator about the Donners, and, following the path he'd cut through the washouts, headed for the mouth of the canyon. Just as I popped out of the canyon, the heavy clouds dumped everything they had. The only place I've seen rain come down that hard was along the Gulf Coast.

The flooding that day was regional. A trailer park and several homes were destroyed down on the flats—it was a big deal. It took the road crews a week to clear the canyon road. I never learned what happened to the Donner party. I hope they were rescued before hunger drove them to desperate measures.

Three

Fiddler's Green

Winter Sports

It's the time of year when days are in perpetual twilight, fields are burned brown by winter frost, and patches of snow lay where the sun never shines. Hunched over my tying vise, I sip coffee (in hopes of doing myself a solid) and listen to the wind batter the canvass cover on the swamp cooler. Snow pelts the window above my desk, but I can't tell if it's blown snow or snowing again. It doesn't matter, and I don't care enough to go see. Shadows creep from the corners of the room toward the desk lamp's puddle of light. My dog, Touch, lies at my feet, and I slip my foot under her for warmth—and to keep the shack willies away.

The phone hasn't rung for a couple of weeks, and nobody's been by to visit for even longer. I worry that Touch could starve if

I tip-over, but I suppose she'd eventually start eating on me and happily washing me down with toilet water. I pull my foot out from under her.

I don't *think* I would eat *her*, but once while reading about a mountain man who purportedly ate the livers of Indians, I got so hungry for liver that I went to town to get some for supper. Touch doesn't know about that.

Except for that time we were both trying to lap up spilt beer, Touch has never been aggressive. We get along, overlooking the little things that irritate, like that nasty scooting thing she does on the rug—a maneuver that is difficult to execute, but one I highly recommend for building upper-body strength.

I refill my coffee cup, this time adding a splash of Irish cream (not the imitation stuff you get at the grocery store, but the real thing). Using imitation Irish cream is like going to a topless bar when you're horny, or watching people eat when you're hungry. I'm in for the day now.

I look at the hook clamped in my vise and draw a blank. My fly boxes are full, and the patterns I like to play with have all been played with. I look through my journal for descriptions of flies I wrote down last summer and find one I'd forgotten about—an olive bodied, brown headed, light-winged caddis I noticed crawling on my boot one day. I tie a dozen and stuff them into the box. The phone rings, but I don't recognize the number so I don't answer. I ask Touch if she wants to go for a walk. The wind slams the cooler cover, the furnace kicks on, and she looks at me like I'm nuts.

I look over my list of winter chores: inspect and repair rods, clean and oil reels, wipe down lines and rebuild leaders, tie leaders and flies. Everything is done and there's still two months of hard winter left. It's too early to start jonesing, coming down with the winter blues. Cabin fever actually has a clinical name, seasonal affective

Disorder (SAD), which means they could come and take me away for shock therapy if they find I've been scooting my ass on the carpet.

I put on another pot of coffee and call a fishing buddy to let him know I haven't winter killed. We make small talk about the mountain snowpack and next year's probable stream conditions, and he invites me to have Christmas dinner with him and his family. I thank him for the invite, but we both know I won't go. I don't know why I won't go; it would take too much self-examination to figure that out, but it's nice to know there's a place I'd be welcome. By the time I get off the phone, it's time to walk down to the road and check the mailbox. And I need to take Touch for a walk before she lays an egg.

I get nothing but bills and I stuff them in my jacket pocket, hoping I won't forget where I put them. We walk back to the creek. It's frozen hard enough to walk on now. I'll take Touch for a hike down the creek tomorrow. It'll be good for us to get out and blow the stink off—one of us is starting to smell like an old buffalo. My spirits lift as I start planning the hike. I'll pull out my old ruck when we get back to the house and pack it for winter hiking with camp stove, coffee pot, dry socks, dog biscuits, and power bars. I'll make a fire and build a pot of coffee. Touch can roam around identifying scat while I sit by the fire trying to figure out where I went wrong. But even a day hike can turn into a life threatening event around here in the winter.

A couple of years ago we both broke through the ice. I went in up to my waist, Touch went in up to her nose. The temperature was ten below. We were lucky there was no wind that day. There was a foot of new snow, so I rolled Touch around in it to dry her off. I thought about starting a fire, but we had enough daylight left to get back to the house before dark if we left the creek and headed across country. We made it back in good shape, but it could have easily went south.

It's dark by the time we get back to the house. I pour another cup of coffee and settle back in at the desk. Touch plops down at my feet and lets out a huge sigh. I reach down, pat her on the head, and say, "You can say that again girl."

Dark Currents

I stare at the painting—a mountain stream dressed in autumn colors—reading the water and planning a cast. My dog presses against my leg, and I whisper to her of summer's promise. The mountains have been silently filling up with snow for months, and the backcountry canyons that I love lie hush and dormant. The headwaters are frozen, in some places all the way across, and the trout are hugging the bottoms of deep pools in a state of suspended animation. My neighbors have taken down their Christmas lights, and dumpsters overflowing with cardboard and colored paper have been dumped. The prospect of getting invited to a holiday meal is gone. Fly-lines are cleaned, rods wiped down, leaders built, and flies tied. But the trailheads won't open for another month.

On clear days, cottony clouds hang close on the mountaintops, and I can't tell where cloud stops and snow begins. The khaki cliffs have reddish brown streaks, but I'm not sure if I see them or just remember them. On the benches, snow and cedar create a black and white landscape. The closer ridges are aviation green, the fields by the house, subzero brown. But snowstorms hide the mountains from view for days on end.

During the perpetual twilight of winter, I look each morning to the mountain's slopes to gauge the depth of snow, and in the mirror to gauge the depth of sanity. Come Spring, snows will recede and sunny days will return, but the return of sanity is always a crapshoot.

The wind moans, blasting snow against the window above my desk, rattling loose panes, muffling the ringing in my ears. I can't sleep and have a four-pill headache. The distance between the clock's chimes seems endless; the short, dark days go on forever. Afternoon shadows creep toward me from the corners of the room, whispering black-laced memories that threaten my mind. The chemicals that balance are, indeed, thin.

When the days are dreary and short, the dark thoughts come, floating just under the surface. Life's digestive juices tug at my thighs as I cast waterlogged flies that sink into their murky depths. Out of season anglers who fish the dun waters of the mind must avoid creeling what they catch there and hold the digested fragments of their minds at arm's length before tossing them, like worn out flies, back into the dark currents to be swept away. Maybe that's why I'm a dry-fly fisherman: dries hold my attention on the surface and keep me from looking too deep and getting pulled under.

Some would say my obsession with fly-fishing is at the root of this state of mind (clinically known as seasonal affective disorder) that I call the shithouse blues, but fly-fishing actually healed my broken mind and saved my life.

When I told my ex I wanted to move west to good fly-fishing country, she told me she didn't want to leave her friends. It turned out that it was just the one friend she didn't want to leave.

One night I was sitting on the edge of my bed staring at the forty-five lying on the nightstand. Beside the pistol was a book about a life devoted to fly-fishing, bright mountains, and clear waters. I was only half way through it and decided to finish reading the book. By the time I finished reading, I determined my soul needed an enema, and a life dedicated to fly-fishing was preferable to an eternity of cosmic dust. I hand carried the paperwork through the court system, turned everything that wouldn't fit into the back of my eighteen-year-old pickup into cash, loaded up, and headed west.

I drove straight through, stopping only for gas and coffee. My ex said I ran away from our troubles, but she wasn't there that morning the snow covered peaks of the Front Range rose from the prairie floor and I first locked eyes on them, when I leaned forward and gripped the steering wheel with both hands and had to remember to blink and breathe, when I was afraid it was all a dream and the mountains would vanish, and I'd wake up back in that urban hell next to her. I wasn't running *from* anything, I was running *to* something—life.

The closer the mountains got the faster I drove. I couldn't wait to start living that life I'd read about. By noon of the second day, I was camped on a creek in Utah, a hundred miles from nowhere, a thousand miles from trouble. Deep in the Rocky Mountain backcountry, my flatlander problems vanished. I could breathe again. It felt like home.

Some look on fly-fishing as a metaphysical exercise, as if salvation may be found in its rhythms. I do hope that is true. But I suspect the sport's redemptive powers lie in the places it takes you and how they are received and remembered. So I tuck those colors, scents, and sounds into the pink undigested folds of my brain. They are the floatant that keep the phantom flies of winter dancing on the surface.

When the days are short and dark, and mood is indistinguishable from sky, the puddle of light from my desk lamp, along with my memories of shining mountains, sparkling water, and glistening trout hold back the shadows and keep the demons banished to the corners of the room. I stare at the painting on the wall, and Phantom flies tightly wound with hackles of hope dance on sunny streams of memory. I catch and hold shocking colors, feel the sun on aching shoulders, hear living water, and smell pine-scented mountain air. The gloomy days melt away with the high country snow, and the seasons cycle.

Snow Queen

The trail is marked by hoof prints and pungent piles left by saddle-horses and pack mules, reminders that the elk hunt is on. Just two weeks ago the mountains were decked out in their fall finery. The aspens were still green on the ridge tops, but lower down they shimmered light green, brisk yellow, and burnt orange. Scrub oaks dotted the slopes with living reds, and the aspen's canopy was pierced by alpine firs—the forest greens of the living, and the rusty browns and silent grays of the dead and long dead beetle-killed. But two weeks in the high country can be a whole season, and now the firs' vivid greens stand stark against the white, skeletal outlines of hibernating aspens. The leaden sky, while not yet threatening, feels confining and foreboding. The willows are bare and brown, and the grasses by the creek have turned straw. Frost covers the pine-shadowed ground till noon, and there's a change in the air; it's not quite nippy yet, but you couldn't spend the night up here without a fire. When the sun does break through, if you can get out of the wind, it's warm and pleasant.

It's strange to think how much this little valley is about to change. Any day now, penetrating, joint-numbing cold will settle over the range, and these hushed valleys will gently fill with snow. Brooding mountains will stand silent sentinel till spring, the only witnesses to the struggles of winter kill and the splintering crack of frozen pine.

In a month, to be on foot where I am now would mean certain death. I doubt I would put up much of a fight. There would be an event, maybe a broken strap on a snowshoe. I'd pull off my gloves and fumble with the repair. I'd take too long in the biting wind, my fingers would get numb, and my sweat dampened underwear would begin to freeze—the shivering would start. I'd circle looking for wood to start a fire, get tired, sit down to rest, and wonder where I left my gloves. I'd become disinterested, hear people talking, perhaps call out to them—the shivering would stop. The cold would become hot, and I'd rip at my clothes, lie down in the snow, surrounded by the lost, in the eternal embrace of the Snow Queen.

All of my life she has come to me in dreams, always walking before me, never letting me see her face. She wears a long, flowing, low-cut dress that sparkles like wind-blown snow in moonlight. Her long black hair sways with her stride, brushing alabaster skin, and the muscles of her back ripple, forming shadows and dimples that stay just out of reach. I struggle to catch up to see her face. I know if I could just see her face, if she would just turn around, I'd be able to recognize her and find her—I would know. But I awake with the key to her identity unrevealed.

For days after the dream I look for her, and every long-haired, shapely brunette fills me with hope. She fades for a time; weeks, months, sometimes years go by—then she comes in the night, and the search begins again. But it's a hopeless quest; her beauty cannot be found in the natural world. I came up here looking for her last winter.

I pushed my way in as far as I could until my lungs stung from the crystalized air and my thighs burned from lurching through three-foot deep snow. My breath came short, sharp, and frosted, and my heart pounded in my ears. I had brought nothing with me, no way to start a fire, no power-bars, no water. I looked back and could no longer see the truck, and blowing snow had already covered my backtracks. I knew if I kept going it would be a one way trip.

I had been there many times in the spring, summer, and fall, but the covering of snow was unfamiliar, and the canyon looked new and unexplored. I looked up the snowy pass and made out the trail, only because I knew it was there, an unbroken line of snow that snaked up and out of sight. I knew she must be up there, but you can't see her from the trailhead; she never comes down that far. She stays above the timberline, where snow trails to nothing from wind scoured peaks.

I looked up the trail one last time, hoping to see her on the next rise, afraid that I was too far gone not to see her. I would have followed her, watching her flowing hair swaying over the dimples in her back. We were both young the first time she came to me in a dream, but I have grown old while she remained young. I thought if I could find her we would walk until I was young again and no longer felt the cold. But I have never been able to will her presence, so I turned back, hoping she would come to me again in the night.

I'm certain she must come to others in dreams as well, or they would not have followed. I read about them in the paper. They leave a trail of discarded clothing and are found naked in the snow—always naked. (A phenomenon called paradoxical undressing.)

I read about a thirteen-year-old boy who had been taken from his family, school, and friends to be brought over the mountain and placed in foster care. He was lonely and missed his girlfriend, so he took off one night in a snowstorm trying to get back over the mountain to see her. He left a note detailing his struggle adjusting to his new school, his disconnect with the hardline religious community he'd been thrust into, and his homesickness and loneliness. Search parties were sent out, and volunteers from neighboring counties fanned out with ATVs and horses, but they never picked up his trail. They found him in the spring, curled up under a cedar tree, brittle and bent, shrouded in his pathetic, lightweight jacket—his foster family had thoughtfully provided him with the words of their "prophet." But not a winter coat.

I think people who say freezing is an easy way to go have never been truly cold. I have, it hurts. I've sat shivering, soaked through, unable to feel my hands and feet, unable to think clearly enough to perform the basic tasks necessary for survival. But I got lucky, and the cosmic law of the mountains that demands dumbass come full circle and be fatal was suspended for me that day.

I hope that young man found his Snow Queen that bitter, snowy night, and that her face was familiar when she turned to embrace him. I hope he did not suffer long.

Provo Girl

Most mornings on the Provo are foggy—at least that's how I remember them. It was the kind of fog that feels wet and cold on your cheeks, a dense, snug fog. I fished the river many times when fly fishing was new to me, but there are ghosts in the fog now, at the edge of sight.

I was in the middle of a ninety-nine day fishing trip (I don't remember now why I didn't make it an even hundred), fishing eight- to twelve-hours a day, staying in the river until it seemed like the banks moved instead of the water. Thirty years ago I fished with more urgency than I do now that I live in the Intermountain West and good trout water is only a thirty-minute drive in any direction. I fished hard, so focused on trying new techniques and catching fish that I sometimes failed to see the beauty around me.

It was a Spartan expedition. I slept on a small mattress in the bed of my truck under a camper shell. I had a propane heater, campstove, and lantern; a cooler I restocked once a week with black bread, black forest ham, and black Irish beer; my books, journals, fly-tying kit, and fishing gear; and a couple of changes of clothes.

I made friends with Mike, the owner of a convenience store in the canyon, and when I got reesty, he let me use the shower and bathroom in the back of the store. As a way of thanking him I took his twelve-year-old son fishing every Saturday.

The road through the canyon was a tortuous two-lane then. One of the businesses that thrived in the canyon was a quaint restaurant called The Chateau. I'd have breakfast there a couple of times a week, and when the cold and sleet drove me from the river, I'd retreat there and sit at the counter shivering until hot coffee and clam chowder warmed me back from the edge of hypothermia. The waitress was from back East. She'd bounded around the country until finally landing there. When I asked her why she ended up on that river, in that canyon, she said God had told her to come there. And I believed her.

Each morning I drove to a vantage point above the river where I'd build a pot of coffee and watch the sun slowly reveal the river below. Sometimes the river would be shrouded in mist, and I couldn't tell if I was looking at fog or looking down on clouds. I felt suspended, reluctant to move and break the spell. On those days, I'd sit silently sipping coffee until the sun burned off the mist before stringing my rod and heading down the slope. Yes, God *would* tell people to come there, to that place. It was a place people needed, a place of healing.

One cold, wet afternoon, I stood in stinging sleet marveling at the way the banks seemed to flow by as the current tugged at my thighs and washed gravel from under my boots. I contemplated the delicate balance of chemicals that separate the sane from the rest of us as I took a pull from my, then, ever-present flask. (This was before the pain in my side forced me to rethink the hard-drinking lifestyle of my outdoor heroes, before I concluded that the outcome could well be shoving a shotgun in my mouth and going atomic, a la Hemingway.) Cold shivers and a runny nose finally sent me busting through the willows, heading for my truck and some of the Chateau's hot chowder and coffee.

When I popped out onto the trail, I was surprised to see a small car parked there. The windows were fogged. I figured it was a couple looking for privacy, but as I got closer I heard sobbing.

It was sobbing that—whether you're the one doing the sobbing or the one hearing the sobbing—shakes your soul. The sobs were punctuated by exclamations of, "Oh God!" and "Please!" They were the sobs of a young woman and they had their usual effect on me—I stood frozen to the ground, helpless and confused, wanting it to stop.

I was a young man then, still operating on the grammar-school rhetoric that little girls were made of sugar and spice and everything nice. I still thought it my duty to rescue damsels in distress. (This was before that kind of thinking had me leaning into a few left hooks, before holding a door open or calling a woman a lady would get you branded a chauvinist—before I embraced the loss of feminine mystique and began preferring the company of a good retriever.)

I noticed a pile of cigarette butts under the driver's side window as I approached. I knocked on the window and asked if everything was ok and if she needed help. The window rolled down to reveal a pretty young lady. Her short black hair—not today's short, where gender is called into question, but more of a 1920's bob—was pasted to her lightly freckled cheeks and forehead. Bitter tears rinsed mascara from her hard blue eyes.

"Are you ok? Do you need help?" I repeated.

She asked me if I had a cigarette, so I dug a fresh pack from my coat pocket and handed it to her, telling her to keep it.

Her backseat was stacked with clothes and household items, and it was obvious she was living out of her car. "This isn't a good place for you. It gets cold up here at night," I told her.

"I have blankets. I'll be fine," she replied.

"No, I'm talkin' blue-ass cold," I said. She smiled at that, and I would have done anything to keep that smile on her face.

An empty potato-chip bag and Coke bottle lay on the seat next to her, so I asked if I could get her anything from the store. She thanked me but said she would be okay. "Look," I said, "I know the people who run the store up the road. If you need anything, go there and get it, and I'll take care of it." I pulled a twenty from my pocket, handed it to her, told her to get something to eat, and headed for my truck.

I stopped at the store and told Mike about the girl and asked him to run a tab for her in my name.

I checked on her the next day and saw she had organized her things, and her clothes were now neatly folded in the backseat. Every time I checked on her, I saw her making progress. Later that month, I noticed a newspaper on her dash and could see she had circled places for rent. I also noticed some brochures from the local college. She had a plan.

She often joined me for morning coffee and we'd sit on the tailgate of my truck, smoke cigarettes, and watch the valley unveil from the fog's blank canvas.

The last time I saw her, the car was empty and she was taking care of herself, fixing her hair, wearing makeup. We talked for a long time that day. She told me she'd found a job at a high-dollar restaurant, was going back to school, and had rented an apartment. When I went by the store that night, Mike handed me a twenty the girl had left for me, and I knew then she'd come that day to say goodbye.

They widened the road into a four-lane a few years later; the Chateau, the little store, and the place where we talked and laughed went away. A sadness comes over me when I pass through there now and think of that dusky-haired, blue-eyed girl.

Our last conversation was one I look back on with regret, punctuated by long pauses that left me feeling like something more needed to be said, a conversation that stays on replay when I sit alone on the banks of a high country river, wrapped in a cold, cozy fog.

Last Cast

I awoke to the sound of fat rain drumming on the roof of the camper shell. The heavy taps became a wall of sound that wrapped around me as I burrowed deeper into my warm sleeping bag and drifted back to sleep.

It's the sudden silence of the storm's passing that next wakes me. I crawl out onto the tailgate and look down the canyon at a thick column of rain about a mile away. Farther down, the storm squats on the mountains like a blank canvas, and spiring Alpine firs punch through here and there—unfinished sketches. The upper end of the canyon is bright, green, and fresh. Ghost clouds hang draped against glistening green mountains. The fishing will be good now.

As I begin stringing my rod, I strain to smell the bitter perfume of pine and hear the canyon's silence, but years of welding dulled my sense of smell, and silence now is the echo of nine-pound double-jacks pounding stubborn steel. It's enough for me to know the scent and the stillness are there. I remember.

I remember the first time a trout stream stole my soul one cold, rainy day in North Georgia, and the ten-inch brown that took my fly when I'd fallen in the creek and was being baptized into a new life. I was cold, wet, and happy. I had found something, something that I wanted to be a part of, something that would come to define me. So I kept coming back to be redefined, rebaptized. There's a beginning and an end to everything, though. There will be a last hike in, a last fish caught, a last cast. I was with Ed when he made *his* last cast.

Neither of us knew it was his last cast, but the signs were there. He needed my help getting into his waders that morning, and I watched helpless as he fumbled with his tippet and fly with stiff, swollen fingers until he finally asked for my help. He leaned on me as we moved up the river, his weight frail and light. And we made frequent stops so he could catch his breath. I had to net and release that last brown for him. I thought Ed was too good to die; I think he was too good not to. Two weeks later he was gone.

They say you shouldn't dwell in the past, but you think about things you know, and I know more past than future. So I think about Ed and others who are gone. Like the young man I took fishing because he needed help, and taking him fishing was all I could think to do. I'd hoped fishing would help him as it had helped me. I stood behind him and held his hand as I showed him the roll cast. A few months later—he rolled his car.

I think about an old friend who called one night, lonely and depressed. He needed to go fishing. We talked about wild country and clear water. We talked about special places folded deep into the backcountry and made plans. But he decided to go to sleep and never wake up instead.

The hike in is tougher than it used to be. As I top the hill, I hear somebody chopping wood in the distance, or is it the sound of distant drums? I listen closer and realize it's the sound of my heart thumping in my chest. Below me, a meadow filled with wildflowers of every description and color stretches all the way to the creek.

I try to imprint the scene on my mind as I go for the pack of antacid tablets in my pocket, remembering that a nurse once told me that everybody who came into her emergency room with a heart attack had a pack of them in *their* pocket. I chew on the tablets and wonder if the scalding in my chest is my retirement plan, or the two jalapeño-laced, gas-station corndogs I had for supper last night. It doesn't matter. I'm too far into the backcountry now, and whatever is going to happen will happen without any more help from me. Besides, doing the purple polka on a tapestry of wildflowers doesn't seem like a bad way to go. I can think of a lot worse—visiting angels spoon feeding me as I cast to rising cutthroats in my mind and tapioca dribbles onto my chin. I decide to push on across the creek and up the next hill to give the arteries a good flush.

I think about a life lived giving up no hostages to the pursuit of fortune, choosing only to work enough to keep a roof over my head and take care of my dog. Radio talk-show hosts point accusing fingers—I dropped out, didn't row hard enough when Pharaoh wanted to waterski. I wanted to stay in bright mountains and explore Thoreau's premise that one's surroundings reflect the depth of one's character. I doubt they do. The empty beer cans I see laying around suggest that character is *not* reflected by surroundings. Perhaps character isn't something you bring to wild places. Maybe it's something you find there.

I can see the wooden footbridge—first built by the CCC, now maintained by the forest service—and that last steep hill above it I use as a benchmark to let me know how I'm doing from year to year. There's a stand of aspen beyond, and a waterfall where I want my ashes scattered when I tip over.

I pause, straining to see distant ridge tops through cloudy eyes and prescription glasses. I know the breeze that cools my brow through my sweat-stained boonie is pine scented, and the sounds of the creek sculpting the narrows and diving over the falls drown out the double-jacks in my head. I hear voices and turn expecting to see somebody, but see only the rings of a rising trout below. Something about the shadows under the firs takes me back to my great-grandmother's kitchen on some long ago Saturday morning. I stand on a hill above the creek, silhouetted against a cadet gray sky, suspended between past and present. Lost friends will fish with me again today, here, where place in time does not exist.

The Bend

In the spooky purple shade of late afternoon, when I was tired from the hike in and a day of wading and fishing, when it had that abandon-all-hope-ye-who-enter-here look to it, the bend had always seemed like a good place to call it a day. But the unexplored has magnetism—like that abandoned house on the block when you were a kid—and the bend, cut by water and time, pulled at me.

No doubt it had been fished, but probably not by many. I checked the upper end several times over the years, but it hadn't looked any more inviting than the lower end, so it went unexplored. At least by me. But I just couldn't shake the feeling that I was missing something. It looked like a tough place, though, and the BLM map confirmed it.

I checked the map several times, looking for an easy way in—there wasn't one. The map showed stretches where the canyon narrowed, along with flats that were probably choked with willows. The map also showed several cricks dumping into the main branch from side canyons; on paper the place just looked fishy. Finally, I couldn't take it anymore and determined to sack up and see how far in I could make it.

By taking the left fork at each confluence, I'd circle the mountain and come out on a dirt road a couple of miles above the trailhead. No way to get lost—at least in theory.

It wasn't fear of the unknown that made me stop and turn around all those years; it was not knowing if I still had the nads to get in and out of places like that. The other thing was I didn't know if the fishing would be worth the effort. Oh, I could've asked around, but I didn't want to draw attention to a potential honey hole.

The bend didn't look spooky in the morning light. On the right side, the slope was covered in Alpine and Douglas fir down to where the mountain scrunched its toes into a cliff. The steep left side was crowded with aspen and crags that jutted through the canopy like the broken teeth of a rock monster. A lone pine stood where the slope turned scree and dived toward the thick willows that lined both sides of the creek every chance they got. The creek bounced off the face of the cliff and boiled out through the willows, angry at the sudden change in direction, so wading up the creek had never been an option. It looked like the best way in would be picking my way through the broken teeth on the left, so that's what I did the morning I headed in.

Every year I hear about people falling off trails, having to be rescued or recovered by helicopter. I always wondered how the hell that could happen—as I looked down at the creek from the hillside, thinking I'd gotten myself ledged up, I *knew* how it could happen. People fall from cliffs all the time around here. It's unforgiving country—unforgiving of stupidity, miscalculation, unpreparedness, and hubris. I should confess, though, there's been several times it must have been looking the other way in my case.

I'd foolishly worn hip waders that day, which caused every foot placement to be accompanied by a corresponding pucker. What kept me moving forward was, once I got high enough, I could see an easy way down—if I could just get to it. I squatted and studied the hillside. I still couldn't see around the bend, so I didn't know how much creek I could fish once I got down. The thought of how to get back out hadn't crossed my mind yet. It never does when I'm in that got-to-get-in-there mode. I'll get out—I don't have a choice.

I made it to the creek, found a fishable pool, and played with a riser until it took an Elk Hair Caddis. Catching that little cutthroat took the pressure off and justified the hike in. I couldn't spend much time at any one spot. I'd calculated that it would take me at least eight hours to circle the mountain, but I'd have to hump it.

I hit three beaver ponds in quick succession once I got clear of the fast water at the head of the bend, making the obligatory casts at each before heading up the slope to get above the willows so I could see what lay ahead.

I'd suspected the banks would be lined with thick cover. And I was right. From my vantage point, I could see game trails crossed the creek at several spots, and it looked like I'd be able to make a few casts at each crossing. It's ok to follow game trails on the flats; it makes getting through thick cover a little easier. But you never want to follow game trails up the slope. Elk, deer, and moose have four legs and can go where you can't—and game trails *never* lead back to the truck.

I traveled and fished like that for about three hours until I spotted a bench above where two creeks merged to form the one I was following. Getting above the willows so I could make better time, I headed for the point of land above the confluence.

The right fork looked better for fishing, but I needed to go left to keep heading in the direction I needed to; so, I took the right fork and wound up catching a couple of nice cutts. I pool-hopped along until the creek took a hard right into a side canyon.

The sound of whitewater rumbled from the canyon, and through a gap in the willows all I could see was churning foam and a series of falls and plunge pools. I headed up the slope to glass the canyon with my binoculars.

The steep slope on the right was covered in a thicket of willow, scrub oak, and young aspen. A meadow lay farther up on the right, sprinkled with wildflowers—yellow heartleaf, white yarrow, blue larkspur, and bright red Indian Paintbrush—and dappled in those grassy greens that give the illusion the sun is shining on a cloudy day. I'd be able to move easily through it, but I'd have to cross the creek to get there, and there was no crossing this little fast mover from what I could see. Above the rapids on the left was a fifteen foot cliff. A row of aspen lined the rim, and if I kept the aspens between me and the cliff, if I could find a way down on the other side, I'd probably be okay—too many "ifs." Even if I made it, I didn't think I could come back out the same way. And with the creek too high and fast to cross, the only way out would be a tough pull straight over the ridge. I was too tired for all that, so I turned back, found a good sittin' rock, and thought about stripping down and soaking in one of the plunge pools. I'd come back later in the summer, when the flow would be down and I could make the crossing.

 I found a stout beaver cut and used it to spike my way to the top of the ridge, stabbing, leaning, pulling forward, stopping to get my breath, topping out in a stand of aspen. The dirt road lay below, and I watched diesel trucks belch black smoke as they struggled up the valley with their camp trailers, taking the *Homo oblivious* to their weekend "wilderness" adventures, complete with flat-screens, cold beer, hot showers, and gray water. Some people never peek through their climate-controlled aluminum shells, never see what's around the bend. Somewhere off to the right I heard the distant, irritating whine of an ATV and remembered what an old elk hunter once told me—"Them four-wheeler riders ain't so bad … once you gut 'em."

 Snow dazzled the far ridges—there's never enough nowadays. I shaded up awhile, wondering at the detours, sidetracks, and restarts that put me under those aspens, looking at snow in July, with another canyon to explore.

Left Fork Diary

May 22: Spring in the high country. I'm hiking into the headwaters of the left fork of what was once—until the fire—one of Utah's blue-ribbon trout fisheries. It's a pilgrimage I make every year in the spring as soon as the trailhead opens, to see if I can—and in the fall just before it closes, to see if I still can. It's a place where sunlight plays magically in the aspen's flickering shadows to suggest perpetual Saturday mornings. It's a place where layers of bullshit get scraped down to the raw meat of character, and you can find yourself coming up short. It's a place that dispels vanity by requiring me to look up at ridges I cannot reach. It's a place where I stop, look around and say, "This, this is where I want my ashes dumped when I buck out." And they will be.

I'm just upstream from the burn-scarred section that was closed for two years because of flash flooding that followed in wake of the wildfire. When I called the state biologist to see how long it would take for the watershed to recover, he asked me how old I was, and then told me it wouldn't be in my lifetime.

The fishing sucked after the fire raged through. I hiked in about a month after the fire when the trailhead was closed. I needed to see the damage for myself. A layer of ash covered the bottom of the creek, and it was that ash that sucked oxygen from the water and killed most of the fish.

There are patches of snow on the far ridges today. Grasses are starting to green up, and the high quakies are starting to leaf out, while those closer to the creek remain skeletal. Willow branches are turning maroon, juicing up, coming out of hibernation. It's the time just before wildflowers bloom, when the dominant colors are yellows of dandelion and purples of blue sage. Blue sage isn't truly blue—it's light green and silver mixed with the gray of dead stems, a blend that gives a purple tint from a distance.

I'm the first one in this year. I crossed a snowbank, and the only sumbitch tracks were mine. I'm breathing hard by the time I top the ridge overlooking the main branch of the creek. There's a flutter in the front of my shirt—I hope it's a cicada. It's important that I make it all the way in, unimportant if I make it halfway out. I'd rather do the purple polka up here (if that's what's in the cards). It would be better than the alternative—rotting away in hospice, picking at bedsores and bad food, wrestling with bedpans and visiting angels with bad attitudes. Dying well is the best any of us can hope for.

The fire exposed rock formations and boulders I never knew were there; the ridges along the creek are covered with them. From a distance some of the crags look like quarried stone foundations of ancient fortresses. You have to get close to see they're natural and not manmade.

There's a rock I always stop to sit on. It has patches of black, reddish brown, and dusty green lichen. Some of it looks fuzzy and soft, but I don't touch it to find out. I don't want to damage it. Who knows, it may have been trying to grow here for a thousand years. I worked up a sweat on the way in; the wind is chilly now that I've stopped.

I saw bear scat on the trail. I'm not positive, but it looked like the pictures that came up on Google. Anyway, that's what I choose to think. I saw one in here last year hauling ass over the ridge—nothing runs like that but a bear. I thought a lot about bears when I first came here, not so much now. I no longer bother hollering "bear" when busting through thick cover. I find it intrusive—not to the bears, to me. Ending up bear scat doesn't sound so bad when you think about it; it would be kinda like having your ashes scattered—only with moisture.

I head above the feeders looking for clear water but find the creek fogged up, bank-to-bank high, and running fast. There's no chance of wetting a fly today, so I head back to a familiar spot to eat lunch.

The log is an old friend; I've polished it with my ass many times over the years. The tree fell long ago, its bark long gone, its color a long-dead gray. Big black ants crawl on it, and I take note—I'm always evaluating an insect's worth as trout food. There's a dead owl tangled in the jagged remnants of the roots and I check it for usable feathers—I'm always evaluating a dead bird's worth as fly-tying material. Its wings are pulled back, legs thrust forward, frozen in time. It must have impaled itself diving on a mouse that lives in the log. Its death was sudden. It was a lucky bastard.

By the time I saw the creek was running high and muddy from runoff and unfishable, the hike had become a matter of pride. Even though I won't fish today, I don't consider it a dry run. I'd have still come. I'd come here a thousand times in my mind on those twilit days of midwinter, when snow pecked at the window above my desk, when the dog didn't want to go outside, when spring was a fantasy. It's not about the fishing—not here anyway. Right now you're thinking, "Yeah, yeah. It's the places not the fish. We get it." But if you live long enough to get as good with your fly rod as you think you are, when you break off the hook because the deception is the real victory and laugh out loud at a missed rise, you'll start to satisfy your thirst for wild with the wild beauty around you. Fly-fishing will become the excuse, and your fly rod will keep you from heading off emptyhanded and having to explain to your friends why it's not about the fishing.

The trail out is tougher than it used to be. Well, it seems tougher. I've run into guys up here who didn't look like they'd make it out, and I wonder if I look like that now. I've got a system—I stop at the top of every rise to get my breath and let my heartbeat get back to normal. It gives me a chance to look around.

I stop on a rise to rest and spot a hummingbird sitting on a naked aspen branch. He's here early; he's been thinking of this place all winter, too. He's dressed iridescently to the nines—green hat, purple tie, white vest, and blue tails. We're close. If I reached out I could touch him, but neither of us finds the other threatening. A stiff wind ruffles his feathers, he bobs in the wind, and I speak to him. I thought about that and decided it was a good thing. Thirty years ago I'd have questioned my sanity, but I talk to trout—why not hummingbirds? Maybe I spoke to him to cut through the high lonesome, maybe I'm more aware of them now, maybe I'm just slower on the trail. I feel brighter inside when I see hummingbirds. I wear red bandannas in summer to attract them, and their sudden appearance never fails to clear my arteries. I once had one land on my finger. I wonder if I'll get any credit for that at the pearly gates.

Four

THE OTHER GUY

THE ENVIRON MENTALLY-CHALLENGED

I'd been thinking about this place all winter. It's my hiding place. I don't come here to hide; I keep it hidden, tucked away in my mind. It's where I go when life sucks and I don't like what I see in the mirror. It's a place nobody can take away. It's where I'll have my ashes dumped when I buck out—there, at the old wooden footbridge, where I always stop to rest and take it all in. In that canyon, I do a lot of looking in—and up.

Cottony clouds light up a harsh blue sky and pile up at the rim of the canyon. The ridges are topped with a mix of aspen and pine, and the steep green slopes leading up to them look, from a distance, like well-manicured lawns, easy on the mind. At the timberline, the wind shimmers the quakies, and in the trembling shadows their white trunks are highlighted against dark green pines. Closer, the slopes turn gentle and are dotted with rocky outcrops stained black and rust by lichen, so uniform that you have to look hard to see they aren't the crumbling foundations of ancient civilizations. On one formation, a lone pine has found purchase, and its shade looks inviting. Down by the creek, blue sage, yellow heartleaf, and white yarrow cover the meadows between the scattered stands of willow. The creek banks are cut deep by spring-fed rivulets whose sparkle competes with the sun-dazzled glint of empty beer cans.

I've been preceded by those whom I (in an attempt at being politically correct) call the environ mentally-challenged. For intellectuals, who pride themselves in the ability to rattle off the Latin names of animals, bugs, and fauna—the *inviron ideota*.

When I hike into remote areas and stumble upon discarded worm containers and pop bottles, piles of empty beer cans, and diapers—which are never empty—I start hating people. Based on the number of times this happens, it would be easy to come to the conclusion that the environ mentally-challenged far outnumber people who respect the environment; however, there is no way to tell, as people who travel through the wilderness with respect don't mark their trails with trash. *They* leave no evidence of *their* passing.

I added an empty trash bag to my accoutrements until I found myself lugging full thirty-gallon trash bags around and still not making a dent. The trash seemed to increase as if I were the victim of some kind of curse, like that Greek god who had to roll a boulder uphill for eternity, only to have it roll down the other side when he reached the top. I gave up on the idea of singlehandedly cleaning up the wilderness.

Most of my journeys into the backcountry involve fishing for trout. I feel like an intruder and sometimes wonder if I should confine myself to observation, forego any interaction with the trout, and be satisfied with the beauty and solitude. But that would put me in a camp with moonbats who think human beings just showed up last week and aren't part of the ecosystem. Besides, I like holding living colors in my hand—and releasing them. The difference between humans and other inhabitants of the planet is *we* have the ability to choose how *we* affect the environment. Sadly, many choose to affect it negatively, or they just don't give a tinker's damn.

When I began finding mounds of empty spinner-bait packages with plastic bags clearly identifying them as coming from the gas station just up the road, I suggested to the owner that he unpackage the spinners at the time of purchase and securely hang them from the environ mentally-challenged's lower lip. To his credit, he seemed in favor of the idea.

I sometimes find empty beer cans stacked neatly in the shape of a pyramid. When I come across *these* monuments to ignorance, I'm reminded of the construction companies I sometimes work for that operate on what I call the pyramid principle, i.e., if you get enough primitive people together you can build anything. When enough alcohol has been consumed to the point building a pyramid out of empty beer cans seems like a good idea, you *should* stop drinking. You *could* find yourself explaining why the shore patrol found you lying naked on a sidewalk in Bangkok with a rubber chicken tied around your neck—and that's all I have to say about that.

Some litter seems not only to be accepted but sanctioned by the Forest Service. I'm talking about the paper-plate signs you see stapled to trees, taped to road signs, and propped up with rocks on the side of the road. Curiosity led me to follow one such set of signs marked "Hick's Reunion" for eight miles, finding when I got to the reunion that the signs were, indeed, apropos.

Over the years I've come to accept trash as part of my wilderness experience. That is until last year, when I found a thirty-pack's worth of empties in one of my favorite remote canyons. The camp site was fresh, and I stood there looking around with clenched fists wanting to kick somebody's ass. I didn't see anybody, which was a good thing, as getting into an altercation with somebody that has the strength and determination to hump a thirty-pack that far probably isn't a good idea. I was sitting on a log, staring at the pile of empties, wondering what could be done when it hit me—while aluminum beer cans, plastic pop bottles, and disposable diapers are *not* biodegradable, the environ mentally-challenged *are*. The compostability of the environ mentally-challenged/*compostus imbecillus* increased my estimation of their overall value dramatically. I had an idea for an environmental awareness initiative based not on catchy slogans, colorful posters, or cartoon caricatures of forest creatures but on aluminum baseball bats. Aluminum ... for the ease with which it can be wiped clean of trace evidence.

Anger Management

Appleton has issues. I'm not talking about his cursing and fist shaking when I jump ahead of him to get to the good bend pools, or conveniently leave my wallet at home when it's my turn to buy breakfast or gas. At those times, I patiently point out that these are behaviors all seasoned anglers engage in, which in the name of friendship must be overlooked. I'm talking about tin-foil-hat conspiracy theories and repeated attempts on my life.

When his fly got hung in the top of a pine tree, I watched with concern as he climbed to the top of a boulder, balanced himself on one knee, used his other leg as a counter weight, and stretched out to make several grabs for the fly. If he slipped, he was looking at a twelve-foot drop into the crick.

"Big fish—behind rock—jerked it—out of—his mouth," he explained between lunges for the fly.

"Big fish? Where? What rock?"

"Rock—at head—of pool," he grunted between grabs.

My immediate concern was for his safety, and as my fly settled gently behind the rock I called out, "You almost had it that time. You just need a little more stretch … Just … a little more … stretch," I said between casts.

I'd like to take a moment to clear something up. I deny Appleton's accusation that *I* was responsible for his fall. He slipped off of that rock when he lunged for my throat as I was showing him the big fish I had just landed.

Lately he's been concentrating on conserving tippet material by tying knots with ridiculously short tag ends that take twice as long to tie and require magnifying glasses and tweezers. The other day, as we were stringing up our rods, I found a long forgotten roll of tippet in the recesses of my vest. That fat-happy glow of the well-stocked angler washed over me.

"Hey, check it out," I said. "You're in luck. I just found a whole roll of 6x."

"It looks old," said Appleton, looking at it over his magnifying glasses. "I don't think they even make that brand anymore."

"Couldn't be more than ten years old," I said, blowing the lint off of it.

"I think that stuff has a shelf life."

"Huh? Naw, that's just if it's been in the sunlight. This has been in my vest," I explained as I unselfishly handed him the spool.

Appleton's allegation that it was old, brittle tippet material that caused him to lose those three twenty-inch cutthroats is false. He was setting the hook too hard. I tried pointing this out to him at the time, but he refused to listen and kept lunging for my throat.

Another sign of his descent into madness is the reesty, scruffy, Duck Dynasty look that he thinks is so cool. Unlike Appleton, I *like* the people *I* kiss. His wife was unaware of what was causing the whisker burn until I pointed it out to her. She then initiated a dry spell that lasted until Appleton resumed daily shaving. I'd just like to say that when my fly got tangled in Appleton's chin whiskers on a back cast, it was an accident. His shouts alerted me to the situation, and by leaning back, raising my rod tip, and ripping the fly from his beard I was able to quickly free him up so he could resume fishing. When I kindly thanked him for the whiskers that made my Adams ride nice and high in the water, froth dribbled onto the bare spot on his chin as he lunged for my throat.

At times Appleton's tantrums seem to be tied to his loss of memory. When he thought he'd left his wading shoes at home, I watched him search in vain through his bag of gear and the back of his truck. I tried to help by asking, "You're sure they're not in your bag?" and, "Did you look under the seat?" This caused him to retrace his steps the first few times, but my well intentioned efforts to help eventually seemed only to irritate. "They say the memory is the first thing to go," I good-naturedly pointed out. "They're wrong," he whispered through clenched teeth as the muscles in his neck began to twitch. "The *first* thing to go is the smartass."

With Appleton relegated to fishing from the bank, I was able to outdistance him for the first time since we had been fishing together. It was heartbreaking to look back and see him standing there looking dejected and abandoned. My eyes welled with tears as I waved and disappeared around a bend in the river.

Appleton's reaction to finding his wading shoes under my duffle bag was, in my opinion, over the top, and his charge that I hid them in order to gain some advantage is totally unfounded.

One of the things that got left behind recently was a water bottle. Well, to be more specific, Appleton's water bottle. I saw him set his bottle on the cab of the truck just before we set out, but didn't think it worth mentioning at the time. He didn't notice it missing until he saw me take a cool, refreshing drink from my canteen after our hot, three-mile hike. I coughed and charitably told him I would be glad to share my water with him, but I thought I was coming down with something. Luckily, Appleton relies heavily on my considerable knowledge of outdoor survival techniques, and I was able to advise him that he could safely drink from the crick by straining the water through his teeth.

He soon expressed some regret at neglecting to bring along emergency toilet paper. Fortunately, I had some and told him I would be happy to share with him. I tore off one square of the paper and was handing it to him when he did this rapid movement thing with his eyes and lunged for my throat. It was when he broke concentration to make the attempt on my life that he had what we now refer to as "the accident."

In the interest of being fair, I should tell what happened to *me* last week. While in the middle of the winter doldrums, I decided ordering a new fly rod would be just the thing to lift my spirits, but after the initial excitement upon its arrival, I found my boredom replaced by an overwhelming itch to take it fishing. It would be another month before winter released its hold on the high country, but I figured I could make a quick run up the canyon during a break in the weather and put the new rod through the paces.

It took five phone calls, a promise that it would be a quick trip, and assurances that we wouldn't go in uncertain weather before Appleton agreed to go with me. I picked up Appleton that morning and he immediately started whining about how cloudy it was and how he wished he'd worn another layer of clothes. "You checked the weather reports right?" he whined.

"Huh? Oh yeah, we're good to go."

"It looks socked in up top," he sniveled.

"We won't stay long. If it turns cold, I've got an extra coat behind the seat you can use," I reassured him.

It was an hour-and-a-half drive up to this section of crick I thought would be the perfect spot to put the new rod to the test. I parked the truck into the wind, jumped out, and began rigging up. I pulled the rod from its tube and removed it from the rod sack. I slipped the tip section onto the butt section and checked that the guides were lined up. I seated the ferrules and turned to get the reel—I couldn't find my reel bag. I went back to the cab of the truck and looked on the seat, behind the seat, and under the seat … nothing. I went back to the tailgate and stared at the pile of gear. I had a clear mental picture of the reel bag sitting by my tying desk where I had put it months ago after cleaning fly lines.

By that time, Appleton had rigged up and was a hundred yards down the crick, and it was starting to snow. The wind was picking up so I had to shout, "I'M GOING HOME TO GET MY REEL!"

"What the … COAT!" he shouted back.

I cupped my hands and shouted into the wind, "OKAY, THEN. I'LL BE RIGHT BACK." And if I hadn't gotten stuck behind that snowplow on the way back I would have made good time.

Fortunately, I spotted Appleton on the side of the road in my headlights. I noticed with interest that he'd developed a twitch in his left eye that caused ice crystals to pop off his eyebrow and float down to rest on—and no doubt give some relief to—his cracked and bleeding lips. He was strangely silent on the way home, and it wasn't until I told him I thought the snow that had drifted onto his shoulders made him look Christmassy that he became agitated and lunged for my throat.

Appleton rests quietly on most days now, but remains delusional and continues to blame *me* for his lack of angling skills and questionable woodcraft; however, I will not abandon him in his hour of need—as soon as he's released, I'm takin' him fishing.

It's Good To Be The Guide

The economic collapse of '08 forced people all across the country to launch cottage industries. My neighbors were no exception. They went from peddling eggs and honey to selling chickens and bees, from giving riding lessons to selling horses, and from raising alpacas to selling real estate. *My* first entrepreneurial venture was in herbal medicine.

While walking in the back pasture one day, I noticed an abundance of rabbit pellets. I figured I could sell them to my aging friends as an herbal remedy for dementia, or as a dietary supplement for raising IQ. They looked nutritious, were definitely organic, and the rabbits were wild, so manufacturing costs would be zero. With the right marketing strategy, I'd be in the chips in no time. I test-marketed the "smart pills" on my ole buddy, Appleton.

I gave Appleton an ample supply of smart pills with instructions to take twelve pills three times a day, cautioning him not to exceed the recommended dosage: "You don't want to get too smart too quick. Being a genius is a huge responsibility."

When I called to see if he needed more smart pills, he said, "I don't think these pills work. I'm not feeling any smarter. As a matter of fact—"

"Yours is a tough case. We may have to up the dosage."

"They taste like crap."

"I think they're starting to work. Besides, you can't come off them cold turkey. You have to reduce the dosage slowly over several years," I explained.

My career as a river guide started about a month later, when the FDA took the shortsighted position that rabbit pellets had no nutritional or medicinal value, abruptly ending my career as an herbalist.

I was casting about for my next entrepreneurial venture when I remembered the half-finished plywood johnboat in the barn. I figured with the judicial application of some caulk, nails, and duct-tape I could have the boat shipshape in no time and hire out as a river guide. It sounded easy enough; the river would do most of the heavy lifting, and I already had plenty of excuses as to why fish aren't biting.

I talked it over with my friend Spider, of Spider John's Bait Shop, who sells beer, bait, gas, bootleg Sunday-liquor, and uncertain hot-dogs that fossilize shortly after purchase to double as crawdad bait. He said I could use the bait shop as a base of operations as long as I kept *his* name out of it.

We decided I should make a trial run to get a feel for the river and test the durability of the boat and equipment. "You'll need ballast," Spider told me.

"Ballast?"

"Yeah, something to represent the weight of the sports in the boat, so you can see how the boat handles the rap—uh … faster water."

"Oh … ballast … dead weight. I gotchya. I'll use Appleton. But you know the river, Spider, maybe *you* should go with me," I suggested.

"It'll be better if you use Appleton. You have life vests right?"

"Life vests? Oh, I figured I could make some out of duct tape and old Styrofoam coolers."

"Yeah, it'll be better if you use Appleton. Put in at Big Hole and I'll pick you boys up at Last Chance. If you make it that far, just look for my old red truck. Don't go past Last Chance or you'll wind up in Dead Man's Canyon, and it can be a little rough. There's no way out of Dead Man's except through Red Canyon, and it's even rougher."

"De—De—Dead Man's Canyon?"

"Yeah, it's right after Dead Man's Rock and Dead Man's Chute. Don't worry. Just look for my truck and pull in there."

"It'll be a breeze," I told Appleton over the phone the next day. "All you gotta do is sit back, enjoy the scenery, and fish."

"You've scouted it, right?" he asked.

I figured it would be a waste of time scouting the river, seeing as how we were going to go down it anyway, so I said, "You bet. We're good to go. Spider told me where to put in."

"Spider? What's he got to do with this? That SOB still owes me five bucks for some flies I tied for him."

"Well, there you go," I said. "You can hit him up when he picks us up at the end of our run. You'll get a nice, relaxing float trip and five bucks to boot. Come to think of it, that SOB owes *me* five bucks. I'll tell him to bring our money when he comes to pick us up. I'll pick *you* up in the morning."

I got Appleton seated in the front of the boat and handed him one of the homemade life vests.

"What the *hell* is that?" he asked.

"Life vest."

"That ain't no life vest. I ain't wearin' that."

"Suit yourself," I said as we shoved off.

We drifted along lazy-like for the first couple of miles. Appleton fished, while I worked the boat. But watching somebody else fish is like watching skin flicks when you're horny. I soon had a rod strung up and we were both catching some nice cutts. We were so busy catching fish that we never did see Last Chance, the red truck … or Spider come to think of it.

By the time I saw the water boiling around Dead Man's Rock it was too late. The river had us in its clutches and we were headed straight for the rock at a pretty good clip.

Appleton turned, grinned, and said, "I told you them pills don't work! Gimme one of them vests!" It was a disturbing grin—his lips were peeled back from his clenched teeth like a mule eating thistles—a grin normally associated with psychotic monkeys. I grinned back and handed him a vest as we spun into the chute bisected by Dead Man's Rock.

We kissed Dead Man's Rock passionately as we went by, and I lost track of Appleton until he popped to the surface like a cork when we entered the flat water below the rapids. I was surprised at how well the life vest was holding up and made a mental note to check with Spider about selling them out of the bait shop. "Hang on, buddy! I'll save you!" I shouted. To which he turned, grinned, and struck out for the bank. Appleton is a surprisingly strong swimmer when properly motivated—he almost made it.

He was obviously disorientated, swimming away from the boat like that. It took everything I had to grab and haul him halfway back into the boat before we were sucked into lower Dead Man's Chute. I chalked his cursing, scratching, and biting up to drowning-man's panic and was finally able to pin him against the gunwale with my knee just as we dropped into the plunge pool below Dead Man's Fall. By then we could hear the roar emanating from Red Canyon.

Appleton's on-board antics had become an element for concern—his mental stability had deteriorated; the monkey grin now seemed permanent; he'd become delusional, claiming that *I* was somehow responsible for our predicament; and his frantic attempts to exit the boat were causing us to take on water. While I'm widely known to be long-suffering, caring, and compassionate, my patience was wearing thin, so I beached the boat so he could regain his composure.

Appleton took off across the sandbar like a striped-ass ape. Realizing his escape was blocked by the sheer cliffs of Red Canyon he began hopping up and down, cursing, and kicking sand in frustration. I'd had just about enough, so I informed him that if he didn't calm down he would have to be restrained for the remainder of the trip. That's when he—still grinning—picked up a piece of driftwood and advanced on me with what can best be described as a bughouse shuffle.

Now I enjoy hate and discontent as much as the next man—as long as it's not focused on me. I pointed out that it was *Spider* who'd suggested the trip in the first place, *Spider* who'd endorsed using him as ballast, and *Spider* who'd failed to meet us at the takeout. "Don't worry," I told him. "I'll help you get even with Spider." It was my success in channeling his anger that encouraged me to give up river guiding in favor of my *latest* venture—psychiatry.

The Izaak Walton Angling Society

The domestic chore is a tool of enslavement—an ancient evil first used by Mesopotamian women to keep their men from going fly fishing—which is, sadly, still much in use today. Of the many nefarious forms domestic chores take—painting, cleaning gutters, and roof repairs, to name a few—the most egregious by far is yard work. With its gardening, weeding, trimming, raking, watering, and mowing, yard work alone can keep the unwary angler off the stream for years at a time.

I first became aware of the potential danger of domestic chores one morning as I was resting on the couch, sipping beer, listening to the comforting sounds of my wife getting ready for work. She came into the room and stood over me with fists on hips and the look of a hard drought on her face, telling me in no uncertain terms that there would *be* no more fishing until my chores were done. With that, she handed me an unreasonably long list of chores and stormed out. I checked the calendar to make sure it wasn't April Fool's Day, grabbed another beer, and began planning my day. While looking over the list, it occurred to me that there was a good chance for a caddis hatch on the river that day. *I* figured the best thing to do was go check on that hatch before getting sidetracked by chores.

After the divorce, I realized just how much fishing time had been wasted on domestic chores and threw that yoke off entirely. In no time at all, I had healthy stands of sage, thistle, dandelion, morning glory, and tumbleweed—hardy perennials that require virtually no maintenance. The only problem I ran into was with the tumbleweeds. They tumbled—on to my neighbor's well-manicured lawns—spreading seeds, hate, and discontent. But the benefit of having more time to devote to the life-enhancing pursuit of fly fishing far outweighed those concerns. My married neighbors, however, remained shackled to their garden tools and lawn mowers. It was heartbreaking to see their sad faces as they toiled away as I laughed and waved to them on my way to the river. I spent many a sleepless night contemplating their plight.

I had long been aware of the spiritual nature of fly fishing and how the rhythm of the rod puts you in tune with the rhythms of God and nature. With my liberation from domestic chores and more time devoted to fly fishing, *my* spiritual growth had been remarkable. I felt divinely inspired to spread this "good news."

I formed the Izaak Walton Angling Society for the Abolition of Domestic Chores (I.W.A.S.A.D.C.) and began holding meetings in my garage to plan my neighbors' emancipation. My success in gathering converts to the cause was met with much wailing and gnashing of teeth from their wives—further proof that my message was divinely inspired. I took it as a sign.

Finding myself liberated from gardening duties but still in need of fresh produce, I began going to the farmers market. I found it much cheaper than gardening, and the time saved by not having to plant, weed, water, and harvest was *much* better spent working on my spiritual progress through fly fishing. I would go every Saturday morning, load up on a week's worth of fruits and vegetables, and be on the river by noon. The only problem was the cost to my Saturday morning fishing time; however, once I began preaching my gospel of liberation, that problem quickly resolved itself. The neighbor's wives began greeting me in their driveways by throwing tomatoes, onions, bell peppers, and summer squash—thus making my trips to the farmers market unnecessary, freeing up my Saturday mornings for fly fishing. Which I took as a sign.

My relationships with my neighbors' wives followed parallel downward trajectories starting with the first time I took their husbands fly fishing. The wives noticed a correlation between their husbands' enthusiasm for fly fishing and their dwindling bank accounts, and although I had done my best to minimize the financial impact by selling some moderately used, outdated equipment to their husbands' only *slightly* marked up from cost, I was blamed.

As fly fishing became more and more central to their spiritual growth, my neighbors began sneaking off with me at every opportunity to go fishing, missing at times what their wives termed "life events." Such as, anniversaries, graduations, birthdays, and on one occasion, a mother-in-law funeral—though to be fair, we did swing by the cemetery that day to pay our respects and show off that twenty-four-inch cutthroat to Castretti's brother-in-law. Indeed, their dedication to their spiritual growth had been commendable. I was eventually banned from holiday dinners, barbecues, and all family functions when one of the wives overheard me giving some much needed marriage counseling.

When Liddelberry told me his wife had insisted they go vegan, I listened in horror to his tale of life without cheeseburgers, bacon sandwiches, and three-meat pizza. I could tell by his sunken eyes, hollow cheeks, and shallow complexion that he was already in a weakened state and in immediate need of my expert intervention.

I told him to get six cases of beer and four cartons of cigarettes and go home and put them by his favorite chair. Then I told him to strip down to his skivvies, sit in the chair, drink beer and smoke cigarettes, throw the empties on the floor, and crush the cigarette butts out on the carpet. "Don't shave, bathe, or go to work," I advised. "After about three days, she'll leave. Then you can clean the place up, take a bath, and eat all the meat you want."

So it came as no surprised when my message of liberation from domestic chores was met with robust, organized resistance.

One night at the garage, I was passing the collection plate when one of the congregation spoke up, "I thought this money was for beer and chips." To which I replied, "Yea verily."

"This ain't beer, it's Old Cincinnati," said Wheedlemire. "How's come we're drinkin' Old Cincinnati and you're drinkin' Guinness? …What's that noise?"

"Sounds like somebody's got a loose fan belt," I said.

I looked out the window and reported, "It's just a bunch of women carrying torches and garden tools."

Peeking out the window, Henman shouted, "IT'S OUR OL' LADIES!"

"Fear not, brethren," I said. "We have nothing to fear from these women if we stand united in our convictions. Somebody hit the lights ... brethren?" When I turned around, the brethren had vanished, having fled out the side door.

The women marched in single file and informed me that their husbands would no longer be allowed to "come out and play," as they put it; there would be no more garage meetings, no more consuming alcoholic beverages without adult supervision, and no more fly fishing when there was work to be done. Furthermore, I was to stop filling their husbands' heads with nonsense about freedom from domestic chores, which they called "duties." In short, I was to cease and desist. I was horrified and filled with righteous indignation at such heresy. I pointed out that fishing, especially fly fishing, was a holy pursuit essential for spiritual growth, and that their husbands were following in the footsteps of the Apostles. I told them to "let my people go fishing." ... But I think it was when I said something about fly fishing for Jesus that things got ugly.

They threatened legal action, property damage, and bodily harm: they said they would report me to the authorities (apparently there was some outdated law still on the books concerning property upkeep and bringing down surrounding property values); burn down my garage (a particular focus of their anger for some reason); and stomp a mud hole in my butt. Bulging eyes, crazed grins, and rage-flared nostrils danced hideously in the flickering torchlight, and I longed for the good old days—when heretics were burned at the stake.

All great spiritual leaders and thinkers have, at some point, been persecuted and had their movements driven underground. I was to be no exception ... I took it as a sign.

Prioritize, Prioritize, Prioritize

Of the many skills that must be mastered in fly-fishing, the most important and useful is the skill of prioritization, an attribute, once honed, that can be used in every aspect of life to ensure proper balance when allocating time and finances to the pursuit of the sport.

Correct prioritization, achieved through the application of logic after a review of the facts, is quite useful in the acquisition of the best in sporting equipment, without which fly-fishing cannot properly be pursued.

Let's say you find yourself in need of a new fly rod (cost: $1,500.00), but it has been brought to your attention that your house is in need of new shingles (cost: $1,500.00). Using the fundamentals of prioritization, the proper priority can quickly be determined. First, review the known facts surrounding the case in question: (a) The roof is not currently leaking, and rain is not forecasted for the immediate future. (b) You will need the new fly rod for fishing long before the roof actually starts to leak. (c) The new fly rod will greatly enhance your ability to catch fish, which can then be eaten, increasing your capacity to provide for your family (a circumstance that can be pointed out once the roof *does* start to leak). Logical, right-minded thinking should now justify the purchase of the fly rod and place it at the top of your list of priorities.

Similarly, let's say your wife's car is leaking oil, and the cost of the engine repair would impact your bank account in such a way as to make the purchase of a new fly-tying vise prohibitive. The application of logic after a quick review of the facts should put things in perspective: (a) The engine repair can be moved lower down your list of priorities by simply instructing your wife to add a quart of oil to the engine when the level gets low. (b) At some point, she will be adding oil frequently enough to make periodic oil changes unnecessary. (c) This cost savings can then be applied to a new tying desk, as well. This method of prioritization can be used in acquiring most all angling accoutrements. In fact, this method can be used to place just about anything into proper perspective.

Say you've been asked to pick up a gallon of milk on your way home from work, but when you get to the store you realize that you only have enough money for that six-pack you've been thinking about since noon. Again, review the facts: (a) You know you will need the beer *long* before you get hungry and need a bowl of cereal. (b) You know that you can go longer without food than you can water. (c) You know that beer is 90% water. The priority of your purchase should now be clear.

The other thing you need to pursue the sport of fly-fishing is time, and prioritization is even more useful in securing that valuable commodity.

Work is often the most formidable obstacle to having the proper amount of time available for fishing. Having no control over the perceived notions of importance others may have, you may find yourself working for a guy who expects you to cancel a fishing trip just because things get a little hectic at work, a guy who puts profits above the happiness of his employees, a guy who is—and not for lack of a better word—a jerk. Quickly review the facts: (a) You were looking for a job when you found that one, so nothing from nothing leaves nothing. (b) Nobody lies around on their deathbed wishing they could spend one more day at work. (c) The extra time you will have on your hands after you're fired can be devoted to fishing. By applying this line of reasoning, the correct course of action can now be taken with a clear conscience.

Social gatherings are another big drain on fishing time. Many of these will be in-law events that are obviously low-priority in nature (such as reunions, anniversaries, birthdays, and holiday dinners). Quite often these events can be avoided by feigning illness or simply lying your way out, which can be justified by, again, a review of the facts: (a) They never liked you anyway. Remember how your mother-in-law shook when she kissed you at your wedding? And how it reminded you of the Corleone kiss of death? (b) People like that don't die, so you'll unfortunately have many more opportunities to attend in-law events in the future. (c) Your absence will be looked upon favorably by most everybody concerned; however, there may be those whose judgment will be clouded due to their close association with these people. Note: When prioritizing in-law events, positive outcomes have a much greater probability of success once all hope of domestic tranquility has been abandoned. Prioritizing social events involving your immediate family can be a bit trickier, requiring more in-depth analysis of the facts.

For example, your daughter is getting married and has unwisely chosen a date for the wedding that conflicts with opening day of trout season. A review of the facts will quickly put things into proper perspective: (a) You know the divorce rate is currently at 75% (give or take), and from personal observation, you suspect it's likely to go higher. (b) This is probably just one of your daughter's many weddings, so you can go ahead with your fishing plans with the understanding that you will attend one of her future weddings. (c) She never liked you anyway.

There's a cosmic order, or balance if you will, to the life events that present themselves for our attention, which can often be maintained by simply doing nothing. I call this self-prioritization, a process by which situations are simply ignored until the natural selection process allows the most important one to rise to the top of the priority list before action is taken. This method works well with domestic situations, which, if ignored long enough, very often resolve themselves (a process called self-resolution). A case in point would be the time I was preparing for a three-day float-trip.

I was packing my gear when I detected an atmosphere of crop-failure permeating the room and turned to find my girlfriend standing there with her arms crossed tightly over her breasts and her foot tapping like a jackhammer. Note: *This* particular body language is indicative of a situation that cannot possibly get worse. Your best course of action at this time is to move forward with your plans in the hope that the problem resolves itself during your absence.

I said, "I thought you were at work."

"We need to talk," she replied.

"What about?"

"US!" she said, thrusting her index finger in my direction.

"I'm good. Hey, did you see what I did with that spare 4-weight line?"

Just before dropping into the canyon and losing cell-service, I texted her, telling her I was looking forward to having our talk when I got back and reminding her the next day was garbage day and she needed to haul the can down to the road. I returned home three days later to find she had moved out and the situation (whatever it was) had resolved itself.

Warning: While the methods of prioritization discussed here are indeed useful, they should not be employed by anglers with moderate- to low- levels of testosterone.

Stuff

If you're new to fly-fishing, the first thing you must wrap your head around is you need lots of stuff. And to be successful, you need to spend as much money as financially possible on this stuff. A lack of stuff leads to feelings of inadequacy on the stream that extend beyond fly-fishing into your personal life. This will be made clear to you by the proprietor of your local fly shop.

They have lots of stuff at the fly shop, and all of it is essential for fishing success and creating the image that must be projected on the stream, the image you have in your head of what a fly fisherman is supposed to look like—tweed jacket, floppy hat, wicker creel, bamboo rod, waders, and fishing vest.

The first thing you need to purchase—even before a rod—is the fishing vest. You need the vest because it has lots of pockets for stuff. It has pockets in front, pockets in back, hidden pockets, side pockets, and inside pockets all of which, regardless of the financial pain, must be filled with stuff. Do not concern yourself that in your ignorance you'll purchase too much stuff—between the pockets are hooks and tabs from which to hang the stuff that won't fit in the pockets. Remember, just as there's no such thing as enough money, there's no such thing as enough stuff. The owner of the fly shop will gently guide you through the selection process.

The most important thing you will learn from the fly-shop proprietor is if you are not catching fish, if you are not catching big fish, if you are not catching lots of big fish, you either don't have enough stuff, or you don't have the right stuff. You've heard of the right stuff. They even made a movie about it, but they got it wrong or something because there wasn't a thing in the movie about fly-fishing. The right stuff is, of course, the stuff you don't have. At some point, the proprietor of your local fly shop will reveal to you the cosmic law of stuff—the more expensive the stuff, the better the stuff.

You'll need the stuff you are going to use ... and backup stuff in case you lose stuff. And all this stuff must be changed out with new stuff periodically. Eventually, your weekly trip to the fly shop on payday will become a sacred ritual, the fly shop your Holy of Holies, and the guy behind the counter full of stuff your personal holy man. His declaration, "I've got just what you need right over here," will become your mantra, and should you unwisely leave the shop without buying the stuff he suggests, it will burden your soul day and night, haunting your dreams until you go back and do the right thing and buy the right stuff.

You will never be able to have all the stuff you want or need, nor will you be able to explain or justify your thirst for stuff. People will tell you that you can't take your stuff with you when you tip over. But that's not true. This will become clear to you when you start thinking about who to leave your stuff to—certainly not your son (the one who finds self-expression through sleeping on his mother's couch and night-shitting his ex-wife's porch), and not your grandson (the one with the pink Mohawk, eyebrow ring, and tattoo of Chaz Bono on his butt cheek). You will make arrangements with your holy man to have your stuff cremated with you and scattered in a secret, sacred setting—in the alley behind the fly shop.

Significant others will mumble under their breath against you and your stuff, going so far as to claim you're spending too much on stuff. This, of course, is nonsense—you must never allow anyone or anything to come between you and your stuff.

One of the coolest things about fly-fishing stuff is it's seasonal—you've got your spring stuff, summer stuff, fall stuff, and winter stuff. Fly-fishing stuff is geographic, as well—there's your lake stuff, reservoir stuff, tail-water stuff, river stuff, creek stuff, and crick stuff. There's even stuff to make more stuff (yes, you can make your own stuff, but for that you need the stuff to make stuff with). Then there's task-specific stuff.

You'll need dry-fly stuff and nymphing stuff, stuff for fishing from the bank and stuff for fishing from a boat, and you'll need stuff for fishing from a float tube and all the stuff for that. There's no chance of running out of stuff you need. There are legions of

Chinese children laboring away night and day manufacturing more stuff at this very moment.

You'll need stuff to wear while you're fishing, as well. The stuff you wear must reflect your status as a fly fisher. And have lots of pockets for you to put stuff in. Fishing apparel is seasonal and geographic as well—there's really no end to it.

Eventually, you'll need an extra room for your stuff, a place where you can lay it all out on the floor and look at it, touch it, hold it, admire it, get naked and roll in it. You will lock this room ... because you don't want people touching your stuff ... because it's yours ... all yours.

Instead of fishing, your prime motivation will become the accumulation of stuff, and you will begin operating in the dark underworld of stuff. You will wind up with so much stuff that you'll sell stuff on e-Bay in order to finance the purchase of more stuff. Your wife will say you don't need any more stuff—and you'll hate her for it. You'll go to the fly-shop and *demand* to buy stuff. You'll get catalogs in the mail filled with the newest and best stuff, and you'll look through them longingly and lovingly. And you will order stuff. (There will be khaki-chick-magnet cargo pants in these catalogs, with lots of pockets ... for stuff.) The stuff you order from this catalog will be obsolete by the time the next catalog comes out, but you *must* purchase stuff from *this* catalog in order to stay on the current mailing list.

When your vest induces hernias, when you can build fly rods out of the back of your truck, when you can set up a fly-tying operation on the bank of a creek ... you're almost there.

In an effort to stay up-to-date on equipment, fashionable with attire, and current on catalog mailing lists, anglers often find themselves adrift in a back eddy of slightly used, outdated stuff. Seasoned anglers are able to turn this to their advantage by cycling this inventory through unwary fishing buddies—slightly marked up from cost (a finder's fee if you will)—generating a self-sustaining revenue that can then be used to purchase more stuff.

Afterword

Why

Fly-fishing is my excuse for getting into the high country and away from people. Antisocial? ... Maybe. I prefer anti-bullshit.

In the high country, I don't have to listen to it, watch it, and digest it to form bullshit opinions based on it. In the high country, nobody's trying to sell me gold, insurance, reverse mortgages, or magic pills—telling me my life sucks because I don't have two bathtubs and erectile dysfunction—while warning me to seek immediate medical attention should I get an erection that lasts longer than four hours ... right. (I'd be calling *The New York Times* first.) In the high country, nobody's trying to sell me blood-pressure medication with side effects: "Heart failure that could result in death ... and erectile dysfunction." (I think I'll just let the high blood pressure play out. Thank you very much.) In the high country, I don't think about those poor bastards below who sell all they've worked for to buy $750.00-a-pill extended life. No thanks. As much as I'd like more time to enjoy cutthroat trout, fall colors, and mountain streams, I refuse to prolong the process of bucking out in order to enrich some greedy flatlander.

In the high country, I can be where neither the bull nor I matter in the overall scheme, where my pathetic interpretations of the beauty around me fall short of reality, where the blank canvas of my mind as I stare at snowy peaks outlined against a hard blue sky with no thoughts invading the landscape is reason enough to have made the climb. And now that I'm a seven on a scale of one to dead, I regret not having come to the party sooner.

I regret wasting over nine years of my life on active-duty service to an ungrateful nation. I regret wasting my youth chasing the dollar, trying to conform in a society based on greed and stuff while wishing I was someplace else; I just wasn't sure where that was until I came to the mountains, felt at home in their wild places, and learned to reap the reward of solitude's solace. I regret wasting so much time chasing tail when the love I needed was better provided by a good retriever. I don't hate people, I just prefer the company of a good dog. There's no bluster or pretense to them, and unlike people, who put conditions on love—I'll love you no shit till you get old, fat, and bald … or I run off with Mr. Buck Naked—dogs love you unconditionally … no matter what kind of an asshole you are. Oh, I've got human friends, but not many. My father told me I needed at least six friends, as it took six to carry your coffin. But I realized that I could be cremated and cut that number down to one—which took a lot of pressure off me. The mountains, retrievers, and trout give and ask nothing for their lessons on love, humility and unselfishness.

In the high country, I found something of spiritual value. At first, it seemed to be always just on the other side of the creek, just on the other side of the mountain, just on the other side. But after making a few crossings and topping out on a few trails, I found it. It was humility. And I found that o-plenty.

I couldn't be anything *but* humble while wondering how the hand of time formed mountains, watching a flash flood bear down on me in a burn-scarred canyon, or holding the throbbing colors of a cutthroat trout in my hand. In the high country, I'm a passing shadow in a state of grace with no value other than compost, and I take comfort in that.

Why fly-fishing? Fly-fishing keeps me from becoming a mountain-top-monk in sackcloth and ashes. And treble-hook dredgers, corn soakers, and stink-bait aficionados were conceived *without* benefit of clergy—and *my* parents were married. That's why.

Fly-fishing is honest; you have to do so many things right to catch an honest trout. Trout rise honestly to the fly, respond honestly to the set of the hook, fight honestly for their lives, and honestly haul ass when they're released. When fly-fishing, I'm the deceiver. But it's not the same as deceiving a trout with a gooey glob of stink bait. And although fly-fishing is based on deception, I find it a much more honest pursuit than most other human endeavors.

In the high country, there's no cell service, and I make it a point not to tell people where I'm going (mostly because I never know myself). I usually go alone. The quiet beauty of the mountains is companion enough. I'm alone, but never lonely—there's trout, birds, and ghosts for company, and laughing streams, whispering aspens, and distant echoes of lost loves for conversation.

I learned at an early age what I perceived as tangible, permanent, and necessary were shadows that flittered away in a moment, never to return, hard to remember once gone. But human beings are narcissistic. We think our shit matters when it doesn't, not really. We all go out the same way we came in—with our ass hanging out (ask any funeral director). Nothing matters to the mountains, and that's the point. That's what I learned fishing mountain creeks and finding the rhythm of a handmade fly rod, a rhythm that seems in tune with the bubbling streams, pulsing cutthroats, and beating of my heart. I learned patience, as well, fishing for the mountain's little creatures of color. I take time, close my eyes, listen to the sound of water, smell the bitter scent of pine, and feel a fresh cleansing deep inside. But it's too much to ask for a clean soul at this point ... I've learned honesty, too, you see.

I learned to hate the flatlands with its loudmouth political pundits— "great Americans" who must be congratulated on their cheaply purchased patriotism. I learned to escape the guy who needs more fiber in his diet, the guy who tells me I'm uninformed and my money will soon be worthless and I need to buy gold from people who will gladly take my soon-to-be-worthless money in exchange for that gold. They care nothing for mountain streams that have no gold but the spawning colors of native cutthroat. They don't care if trout have water to live as long as they have water to grow pistachios and brew beer, as long as they make enough flapping their jibs and selling gold to afford the next trophy wife. But they don't understand me any better than I understand them.

I didn't want to work, work, work until I dropped dead in harness—like my father. I got tired of doing labor that enriched others and left me living hand-to-mouth. I walked away, working just enough to finance my addiction to fly-fishing and high-country trout. And the rich got richer without me. Realizing I didn't matter was liberating; I was free to turn my back on the well-worn path to mediocrity. Mediocrity seems an impossibility in the high country, where nothing is mediocre.

In the high country, I find no evil. Oh, bear *will* eat you, moose *will* stomp you, and unpredictable mountain weather *will* kill you—if you've got your head up your ass. But none of that is evil. Evil, as I understand it, is greed and must be manifested by people. And when I'm away from people, I'm not exposed to their evil, not exposed to those who worship the brass bull in New York City, or tithe at the big-box chain store. In the high country, I can still find places resource raiders haven't pillaged, but that's only because it isn't cost-effective to do so, or they would. And they will.

I was never able to strike a balance between my spiritual needs and the requirements of society, so I chose solitude, trout, and mountain streams. But there's more to that story. And I won't bore you with it, or do injustice by presenting a one-sided version of events that led me to that choice. In short, I'd made a mess of human interactions and reached a point where I had to cut bait or bail. So I bailed.

Of course there are times when I wonder what my life would've been like had I stayed in play, cured a disease, built a pyramid, or developed a more destructive bomb. But I'm glad I didn't.

Acknowledgments

I'd be remiss if I didn't mention the two people who helped me put this collection together. For his long standing friendship and patience in reading my pathetic attempts to write, I'd thank my trusted reader and oldest friend Russel Pouncey. For her patience and expertise in editing, I'd like to thank Lisa Ricard Claro, a well-established author in her own right, who walked me through the jungle of syntax and encouraged me to be all I could be as a writer of rambling thoughts and stuff nobody cares about.

www.ingramcontent.com/pod-product-compliance
Lightning Source LLC
Chambersburg PA
CBHW060815050426
42449CB00008B/1670